P9-DWG-606

What No One Ever Tells You About

STARTING YOUR OWN BUSINESS

Second Edition

Jan Norman

Dearborn™
Trade Publishing
A **Kaplan Professional** Company

This publication is designed to provide accurate and authoritative information in regard to the subject matter covered. It is sold with the understanding that the publisher is not engaged in rendering legal, accounting, or other professional service. If legal advice or other expert assistance is required, the services of a competent professional should be sought.

Vice President and Publisher: Cynthia A. Zigmund
Acquisitions Editor: Michael Cunningham
Senior Project Editor: Trey Thoelcke
Interior Design: Lucy Jenkins
Cover Design: Scott Rattray, Rattray Design
Typesetting: Elizabeth Pitts

© 1999, 2004 by Jan Norman

Published by Dearborn Trade Publishing
A Kaplan Professional Company

All rights reserved. The text of this publication, or any part thereof, may not be reproduced in any manner whatsoever without written permission from the publisher.

Printed in the United States of America

04 05 06 10 9 8 7 6 5 4 3 2 1

Library of Congress Cataloging-in-Publication Data

Norman, Jan.
    What no one ever tells you about starting your own business : real-life start-up advice from 101 successful entrepreneurs / Jan Norman.—2nd ed.
        p. cm.
    Includes bibliographical references and index.
    ISBN 0-7931-8596-3
1. New business enterprises—Management. 2. Entrepreneurship. I. Title.
    HD62. 5 .N68   2004
    658'.041—dc22   2004006708

Dearborn Trade books are available at special quantity discounts to use for sales promotions, employee premiums, or educational purposes. Please call our Special Sales Department to order or for more information at 800-245-2665, e-mail trade@dearborn.com, or write to Dearborn Trade Publishing, 30 South Wacker Drive, Suite 2500, Chicago, IL 60606-7481.

DEDICATION

To my husband, Mark Landsbaum,
my ever-present help and inspiration.

CONTENTS

PART 7 THE INTERNET 157

PART 8 START-UP GUIDE 183

PREFACE

If you are thinking about starting a business—or if you already have started one—this book is your opportunity to learn from those who went before you. This also is a book of surprises—101 of them. One thing is for sure: The 101 business owners in this book wish *they* had known about these surprises in advance.

I asked hundreds of business owners this question: If you could start all over again, what would you do differently to be more successful, to be successful sooner, or to be successful with less effort? From their stories, I chose 101 to share with you. This second edition has 35 new stories, including Sergey Brin of Google, Paul Orfalea of Kinko's, Doris Christopher of The Pampered Chef, and Robert Basham of Outback Steakhouse. Plus, there's a new section about the Internet. This is your chance to benefit from their hindsight. When you've finished reading this book, you will know what they didn't when they started out. You should also learn a heartening lesson. A mistake or surprise doesn't have to kill a business if you make the necessary adjustments and don't give up.

These experiences are not flukes, nor are they isolated to certain industries or regions. The 101 people and businesses profiled in these pages are drawn from every region of the country. Their ventures touch every industrial category. The businesses range from one-person, home-based offices to billion-dollar global corporations. The youngest owner was in his early 20s when he began. The oldest was in his 60s. They are men and women, minorities and immigrants, the rich and the merely rich in spirit. Despite their diversity, they have much in common. If you're a budding business owner, they share this bond with you, too.

Sooner or later (and probably more than once) you will be surprised by something you did not anticipate when you decided to go into business.

Each of these people was. In fact, I've interviewed thousands of business owners in the past 15 years, and they all tell stories of being surprised after entering the wonderful world of entrepreneurship because they didn't expect—or no one ever told them about—*something.*

I'm certain you will find a useful tip, a helpful insight, or at least a warning sign in these stories. In fact, I'm certain you will find more than one.

However, you won't learn everything about business ownership in these pages. Some stories may not relate to you or to your business directly, but if only one of the 101 is helpful, you just might be more successful or not have to work so hard before achieving success. At least that's what each of these 101 business owners told me. (Imagine how successful you could be if 10, 20, 30, or all 101 of these stories help you!)

Other than the fact that each person profiled here was surprised by the unknown, another undercurrent runs through all 101 stories. It is the irrepressible will to succeed—something seemingly so rare these days, yet nearly universal among successful business owners. Success did not come easily to any of these entrepreneurs. Each faced challenges; many faced multiple setbacks; some failed miserably before succeeding. But each had the will to press on, to achieve a dream, to reach a goal.

You will find that some of the 101 business owners solved their problems by doing the very things others found to be of no help at all. Circumstances and personal style will dictate what works for you, as they did for these business owners. Yet in this potpourri of wisdom and experience, you are bound to find something helpful.

When you do, don't thank me. Thank these 101 business owners who braved the harsh realities of commerce and emerged better for the experience. They are generous in spirit. They were happy to share their hard-learned lessons, because in doing so they might help others travel that road more comfortably. My advice to you is this: Take advantage of their gift.

I have arranged their stories in seven parts. Start with ways to use advance planning to avoid problems down the road; move to early, critical threshold decisions you need to make when starting a business; next discover the costs and sources of capital; then examine how to develop a boss's know-how and perspective; after that learn where help awaits and how best to use it; and explore winning approaches for marketing your business. This second edition contains two important additions: a new section of real-life experiences of starting Internet businesses and a new section on applying the 101 lessons to your own business.

If you absolutely cannot tolerate the unexpected and shy away from challenges, you probably should not go into business for yourself. Successful business owners will tell you that surprises are the challenge, not the penalty. Learn from these veterans of the business world. Be forewarned and forearmed. When surprises surface, be ready to adjust and move forward. After all, the uncertainty of business ownership is a great part of its wonder—and its fun.

ACKNOWLEDGMENTS

I want to thank all of the business owners who took the time to tell me about their business start-up experiences, but especially those business owners featured in this book.

I appreciate the assistance of my brother Jim Norman, executive director of the Phoenix Creative Planning Centers Foundation, Inc., the U.S. Small Business Administration, and National Association for the Self-Employed for finding business owners who willingly shared insightful and useful lessons they learned through starting their own companies.

PART 1

LOOK BEFORE YOU LEAP

■ ■ ■

You've got this seed. Some people describe it as a burr, an itch, or a passion. You want to start some venture to scratch the itch or realize the passion.

No one ever told you how much planning you need, where the money would come from, how much you should know, or whom to ask if you don't know. What the experts do tell you just may be wrong. Wow! This business stuff is hard, but nobody ever told you how hard. And you haven't even hocked the house yet.

Before you run off and do something you'll regret, take a deep breath and think about what you need to launch your enterprise successfully. If you don't have enough information and market research to point you in the right direction, now is the time to get it.

Write—yes, *write*—a business plan. If that plan has some holes, ask more questions, study more spreadsheets, and look at more possible locations.

The pre-start-up phase is the time of greatest impatience for the new business owner. You're eager to run. Just be sure you know where the track is.

After you've prepared and have that sense that your idea and the timing are right, trust yourself to make it happen, even if the supposed experts can "prove" you're wrong. Now is the time to do it.

1. IT ALL STARTS WITH A DREAM

The hardest part of start-up is summoning the will
to do whatever it takes to make your dream reality.

■ ■ ■

For years, when television viewers thought of Wendy's International, they didn't think of the freckle-faced, red-haired girl that was part of the logo for the fast-food hamburger chain. They thought of Dave Thomas, the company's founder who appeared in Wendy's commercials. Few burger fans knew that Dave made his first million dollars as a Kentucky Fried Chicken franchisee. He even invented the rotating bucket sign that stood over thousands of KFC restaurants for years.

But when Dave sold his franchises at the age of 37, his dreams drifted back to his favorite food: hamburgers. Fresh meat, slowly grilled, large in proportion to the bun. "Everyone told me—especially bankers and financial people—that opening another hamburger restaurant was a bad idea," Dave said. "They said the market was saturated. McDonald's and Burger King had all the business they could handle, and the world didn't need another hamburger restaurant."

If Dave had listened to the experts, he never would have launched the $6 billion Wendy's, named for one of his daughters. Instead, Dave followed his instincts and his dream. On November 15, 1969, he opened a restaurant in Columbus, Ohio, that served made-to-order hamburgers, chili, french fries, thick milk shakes, and soft drinks. That was the entire menu. The first day, customers lined up out the door. "The other guys sold batch-cooked hamburgers made from frozen beef that sat under a heat lamp," Dave said. "I knew that people would like what Wendy's offered. And, luckily, I was right."

Luck had little to do with it. If you're going to follow your instincts, you'd better hone them well first. Since age 13, when Dave began working in a restaurant, he talked about opening his own business some day. He learned every aspect of the business, from cleaning tables and flipping burgers to focusing the menu and marketing. He may not have had a written business plan and formal market research, but Dave had been creating that plan and gathering information informally for 25 years. "Research isn't everything," Dave wrote in his autobiography, *Dave's Way.* "Not long after we started, Burger King paid a lot of money for a research study that explained why Wendy's wouldn't work." Wendy's did work, Dave said, because it provided what customers wanted—quality coupled with fast service. Dave found that customers were willing to pay more for a good hamburger. Later, when customers asked for an expanded menu, Wendy's, now headquartered in Dublin, Ohio, added salads, baked potatoes, stuffed pita sandwiches, and chocolate chip cookies.

In the beginning, Dave's vision for Wendy's wasn't international. He even continued his executive job at another restaurant chain for a while. Yet his first restaurant was profitable after six weeks. He opened a second one a year later. The chain expanded beyond Ohio in 1972. That's when he quit his other job.

When asked for advice, Dave would say, "It all starts with a dream. The hardest part is being willing to do whatever it takes to make your dream a reality." Dave built Wendy's on some basic rules:

- Do your research. Know the business you want to start. Understand your customers and their needs.
- Your dream must be different in some way from your competitors' dreams.
- Quality and customer service must be your twin top priorities.
- You must work hard.

Although Dave died at the age of 69 in 2002, his advice and Wendy's International live on.

2. HONESTY AND PERSONAL COMMITMENT

Never underestimate the value of honesty in business.
It will be your greatest asset.

■ ■ ■

One reason that Sarris Candies of Canonsburg, Pennsylvania, is a global enterprise selling chocolates and roasted nuts today is founder Frank Sarris's dedication to honesty when the company was small.

Frank started making chocolates in his basement in 1960 to please his sweetheart and future wife Athena. It grew from a part-time pleasure to a full-time candy shop. One of the major revenue streams has been fundraising candy sales for schools and organizations. "I was approached by a group to make a presentation on my products," Frank recalled. "It was a large, prestigious group and getting this account would greatly enhance my business." When Frank arrived to make his pitch, he discovered that he was one of five candy representatives being interviewed. The others were from large companies, so he thought his chance of getting the account was nil. "When my turn came, I laid it on the line. I told them my products cost more and explained why. I told them that I didn't know if I could produce and deliver the quantities that they needed. I told them I would do my absolute best to give them exactly what they wanted, when they wanted, and at the fairest price I could." When he finished, the group's leader stood up and announced, "We're going with Frank Sarris. He's the only one who has told us the truth and has given us his personal commitment to fulfill our needs."

Sarris Candies continued to pursue that strategy over the years, sometimes at the price of losing an account. "If you believe in your product, why lie?" Frank asked. "If you are going to lie, it will catch up with you." Once he attended a large picnic where the company president introduced Frank as "the guy we've bought candy from for years and years because of his honesty." This standard extended to the entire company. Employees could eat all the candy they wanted while working, but not sneak it home in a coat or purse. "Ask me for anything," Sarris said. "I hate stealing."

Frank never intended for Sarris Candies to outgrow his basement. As sales grew, he built a small shop next to his house. Then he tore down the house and built a larger store. The family lived on the second floor to save capital for the business. The candy company that honesty built kept growing into a 120,000-square-foot manufacturing plant and distribution center in addition to the candy shop and old-fashioned ice cream parlor. The place was so busy that during the holidays, four policemen were needed to direct traffic. Busloads of senior citizens came from miles away to shop.

Sarris Candies was sold in grocery stores and Hallmark gift shops in six states, through mail order, over the Internet, and, of course, the fundraisers. In that last area, the company established programs and services to help the groups and schools make the most of their selling efforts. Sarris provided the paperwork and sales incentives. Significantly, as it relates to honesty, the company didn't inflate its prices or cut quantities or quality for products sold through fundraising events. "Our customers are our resources," Frank said, "and by continuing to be honest and offer quality products at fair prices, we have been able to successfully meet the demands of the marketplace and continue a steady, profitable growth."

3.
THE BUSINESS
DOESN'T DEFINE YOU

You are not your business. Don't allow it to control you.

■ ■ ■

Paul Orfalea always figured he'd have to own his own business because he lacked the abilities of a good employee. He was dyslexic, so he never was a good reader or speller. Neither was he technologically adept. As a young graduate of the University of Southern California—barely scraping by, to hear him tell it—Paul didn't know how a Xerox copier worked. He just knew he could sell what came out of the machine. If students would pay 10 cents a copy at the library, he would offer the service for 5 cents a copy. In 1970, Paul borrowed $5,000, rented a 100-square-foot garage near the University of California Santa Barbara campus, and filled it with a copier, an offset press, film processing, and school supplies. He named his shop Kinko's, which was his nickname referring to his curly, red hair.

The shop was instantly busy, and within four weeks he hired his first employee. Paul's attitude from the beginning toward those he hired—he called them coworkers, not employees—was, "I'm so happy you're here; everyone does things better than I do." That's when Paul's goal became working himself out of a job. He turned coworkers loose to serve customers, take risks that would improve Kinko's, and make decisions.

Kinko's grew from one to 128 stores by partnership agreements between Paul and individual store managers. When the company had just seven stores, a manager called Paul, said a customer's check had bounced, and asked what to do. That's when Paul decided to be less accessible. Otherwise he would be chained to the day-to-day operations, controlled by the business instead of being in control. "I expected managers to come up with solutions, not come to me with every little thing," he said. "I was never the manager; I was the owner. I'd wander around, observe what people were doing right, and tell the others about it." When one manager was successful with round-the-clock store hours, other Kinko's followed. Coworkers' risk-taking experiments introduced videoconferencing capabilities, digital technology, company-wide voice mail, and Federal Express drop boxes into Kinko's stores. (FedEx bought Kinko's in 2003.)

On one level, Kinko's was a business that shouldn't have succeeded as well as it has. It lacks proprietary technology. There are few barriers to competitors entering the market. And most customers buy on the lowest price. But because Paul didn't get bogged down in daily routines and doing all the work himself, he could see the big picture that led to growth. "Most business people don't see tomorrow; they see today and yesterday. That's not for me." He took care of the business side of each of the partnerships in the early years so that managers were free to work with customers rather than tinkering with the machinery. Paul didn't perceive Kinko's to be his alter ego, so innovation and change were allies, not threats. "To be successful, you must balance work, love, and play. Your business is an instrument to make you happy. It doesn't define you," Paul said.

Kinko's expanded to 11,000 stores worldwide and $2 billion in revenues. Paul severed management ties with the company in 2000 and sold his remaining ownership for $116 million in 2002. But he didn't retire. He established West Coast Asset Management, Inc., an equity management practice, and the Orfalea Family Trust, which donated millions of dollars to education and charity. As with Kinko's, Paul didn't let these ventures control his time or his life.

4. MAKE A PLAN

A formal, written business plan serves an invaluable,
positive purpose for a new venture.

■ ■ ■

Patricia Creedon seemed destined to own an electrical contracting company. Her father was a construction manager for DuPont, and she married an electrician. Throughout her childhood, her father talked about starting a business, "and he brought me into his dream," Patricia said. "He always said, 'You can be president.' He gave me that entrepreneurial spirit." Although he had sons, Patricia's father always shared his vision with her. Gender bias didn't exist for him. When Patricia finally started Creedon Controls, Inc., in Wilmington, Delaware, in 1989, she was the president and her dad was vice president, even though he lived in another state.

Patricia was so busy incorporating her company, writing the bylaws, and running after customers that she didn't write a formal business plan. "I had it in my head, but there's a big difference in putting it on paper," she said. It was an oversight that almost sunk her fast-growing company.

She worked out of the basement in her home. The daily grind of growing a company while raising three children kept her from meeting with other entrepreneurs to share problems and concerns. Despite double-digit annual sales growth, Creedon Controls was cash poor. After five years, Patricia thought she would lose her business. "I had a good story to tell, but I didn't know it," she said. "I needed money and didn't know how to get it."

In the start-up phase, Patricia had attended a few workshops put on by the Service Corps of Retired Executives (SCORE), a business counseling group affiliated with the U.S. Small Business Administration. She returned to SCORE counselors for help writing her business plan.

A typical business plan details what the business is, how its goods and services are marketed, its financial analysis, and its operations. If the plan is used to obtain financing, it should state how much money the company needs, how the money will be used, and how the company will repay the loan or compensate investors. The plan should describe what the company does and the distinctiveness of its products or services.

Creedon Controls, for example, performed electrical contracting for heavy industrial uses, specializing in robotics and fiber optics. Patricia described the qualifications and responsibilities for herself and her top executives. If she had written the plan when she founded her company, she would have detailed her start-up costs and her five-year plans.

The plan also should explain the company's system for maintaining financial and other records, all insurance concerns, and security measures, such as inventory control. The marketing section should describe the company's potential customers and how to reach them. It should evaluate direct and indirect competition and the company's competitive advantages. Finally, the marketing section should discuss industry trends and how the company will lead them. The financial section summarizes the company's available capital and financial needs. A new company needs a pro forma cash flow statement and a three-year income projection using the revenue and spending information from the pro forma. This is the part new entrepreneurs hate. How can they know the dollars and cents until they're actually in business? That's where research of the industry and competition helps. Books, trade association publications, surveys, and studies contain financial information about similar companies that can serve as a guide. The business plan is the blueprint, not the building. As circumstances change and new information and experience come to light, the plan can be changed. Any documents—executives' resumes, financial analyses, leases, incorporation papers—used to write these four sections of the business plan should be placed in the plan's appendix.

"Writing a business plan got me out of the day-to-day grind and let me focus on the future," Patricia said. "Entrepreneurs need to spend time on the vision."

Her company evolved to focus on the high-tech end of electrical contracting. Creedon Controls installed fiber optics, heat tracing, and sophisticated security systems for offices and industrial plants; and robotics systems for manufacturers. Patricia also prepared a strategic business plan for the future and became active in executive advisory boards, which honed her own skills while allowing her to work for good causes. "I probably got into business at the worst time," she said of the early 1990s, which was marked by severe recession. The construction industry was hurt severely. However, the discipline and written business plan required to survive a poor economy helps an entrepreneur do even better in good economic times.

5. SUDDENLY, YOU'RE NOBODY

Line up plenty of cash and credit lines before starting your business because you may not be able to get them later.

■ ■ ■

Luciano Capote—his friends call him Lucky—knew what it was like to start with nothing. When he immigrated to Texas from Cuba in the 1950s, he was penniless and didn't speak a word of English. He washed dishes for two years and saved enough money to go to Texas A&M University. After he graduated, he got a job with a start-up computer company named Texas Instruments. Lucky advanced as the company grew, and he eventually managed 400 employees. Lucky discovered that banks frequently courted corporate executives with offers of home equity loans and credit cards. Through these offers, Lucky had access to the funding he would eventually need to start his own company. While still employed at Texas Instruments, Lucky did not know how difficult it would be to raise the money once he became self-employed. When he canceled a $50,000 home equity line of credit, it never occurred to him he was cutting off a source of money that would be next to impossible to acquire once he launched his own business.

At age 58, Lucky felt too dissatisfied to stay at Texas Instruments and too young to retire. So in 1984, Lucky took his retirement savings and started National Microcomp Services in the garage of his Tustin, California, home to service computer systems for corporations and public agencies. His prospects were excellent for winning contracts with companies that owned Texas Instruments computers but lacked in-house repair skills.

"I tried to get that line of credit back, and the banks wouldn't talk to me," Lucky said. "If you check that box that says 'Are you self-employed?' on the loan application, the computer will read nothing else." He couldn't even get a line of credit at a large bank with which he had a $120,000 contract to service its automatic teller machines. "People take for granted that they will get a line of credit because they own property, but the self-employed often can't unless they have personal relationships with their bankers."

Many would-be business owners think they'll get their money from banks, but most start-ups finance their dreams through Aunt Edna and the cookie jar—in other words, relatives and personal savings. A study by the National Federation for Independent Business (NFIB) in Washington, D.C., found that 75 percent of new businesses relied on their owners' money. Lucky's cookie jar was his retirement money. Some business owners save for years or work two jobs. One business owner sold his coin collection. Another took a loan on his life insurance policy. Still another invested an inheritance. In the most recent recession, thousands of laid-off workers launched new ventures with their buy-out pay from their former employers. The NFIB study found that almost one third of U.S. businesses receive a financial push from family and friends. Still other businesses turn to helpful suppliers and customers.

Don't let the lack of money hold you back, Lucky advised. Just as he managed to get a college education on minimal resources, he managed to grow Microcomp Services tenfold from his garage days to contracts and employees from Hawaii to Arizona. The company had multimillion-dollar contracts to repair and service computer equipment for the Navy and for major corporations such as Motorola and Data General. Lucky finally got that line of credit after almost five years by turning to a small local bank where the loan officers knew him well. However, even after years of business success, he still had to sign his personal guarantee for business loans.

6. UNKNOWN TERRITORY IS DANGEROUS

Choose a business you know and
with which you have experience.

■ ■ ■

Norris Randall, fresh out of the Army and holder of a college degree in industrial arts, had a job offer to teach high school. Then his father called for help. Louie Randall had owned a successful men's clothing store, but in 1956, he was talked into starting a tile installation business by a guy with big promises: "We can make $100 a day building bathrooms, and we'll split it 50-50." It was not a business father or son knew anything about. If Norris had stuck with his training, he would have gone into woodworking. He had, in fact, built several houses before his father's leap from retailing to tile work. Louie bought a used pickup truck and some materials, and then asked Norris if he'd like to learn the tile business from his expert partner.

"Big mistake," Norris admitted. "It quickly became apparent that the man did not know much about business recordkeeping and the need to make a profit." The partner, for example, didn't bother to figure the cost of materials and shipping into his pricing. After a few months, the tile man was gone, and Norris continued Randall Tile Co. in Phenix City, Alabama, learning on the job. "It was still a seat-of-the-pants operation," Norris said. "I wouldn't do it that way again. I'd have chosen something I had some knowledge of and experience with."

After three years in business, Norris thought the company was doing well until an accountant friend helped him figure his income taxes. "After we figured out that I had made $4,400 for the whole year, he said, 'You might as well go out and get a job.' That's when I realized this was not a game," Norris said. Fortunately, Norris's wife had a nursing job to support the family.

That financial exercise was the wake-up call Norris needed to get a handle on each project's costs. Previously when Norris bid for a job, the customer would claim that a competitor was willing to do the work for less. Norris would meet the lower price to get the work. "I decided, if I couldn't make a profit, I didn't want that job," he said. He stopped meeting competitors' bids and stuck to his own terms. As Norris's reputation grew, customers started giving him the work anyway because of his quality, reliability, and references. Much later, Norris figured out that many of those lower bids were phantoms.

In 1960, after the birth of the Randalls' third son, Norris's wife quit her nursing job to keep the books for Randall Tile Co. Nine years later, the company stopped accepting installation work and concentrated on supplying tile and related materials to contractors. As a supplier with one location, Norris was better able to manage his workforce than he had been with dozens of work sites spread over a wide area. When Norris wanted to cut back his hours, his son, James, took the reins of Randall Tile Co. The small firm still held its own against warehouse retailers. The key, Norris said, was resisting the urge to meet competitors' prices. "One of our biggest customers told my son that we don't have the lowest price, but the competition couldn't guarantee it would have the product, and we could," Norris said. "We always came to the rescue; that's how we survived."

7. OVERCOME IGNORANCE WITH DESIRE

If you don't have experience or business know-how, you'd better want success enough to compensate.

■ ■ ■

Craig Hartman was still in high school when he started painting houses and decided he liked it enough to make a career of it. Not one to work for someone else, Craig started his own company, Preferred Industrial Services, Inc., in Fort Wayne, Indiana, in 1973. Never mind that he had no experience running a business. Never mind that he had no technical knowledge. Never mind that his dad and adult friends told him to go to college instead. "I talked to more than a hundred people during my start-up period," Craig said, "and most of them told me not to do it, I was too young, too inexperienced. I remember only four saying 'do it.'" Craig ignored his doubters, but faced enormous barriers that he overcame only through an absolute refusal to fail and, as Winston Churchill put it, "blood, sweat, toil, and tears."

"Without question, my lack of abilities in technical knowledge and business management significantly impeded my company's growth," said Craig, who resigned as Preferred Industrial Services president in 1998 to start a bank. "You need to have at least a solid foundation of business knowledge or experience so you know what it takes to run a business." Craig's willingness to ask a hundred business people for advice helped him overcome his inexperience. Even those who urged him to go to college instead of starting a business gave him plenty of helpful information. But asking for help was tough. "Type A personalities don't like to admit they don't know everything," Craig said. "I had to make an honest assessment of where I was, a practice that has served me well over the years."

Craig hired workers and outside consultants to fill in the gaps in his knowledge and experience. One old hand taught him how to price jobs. Others taught him the differences in types of paint. "Fortunately, I had solid sales skills," he said, "but the toughest sale was to get people to come to work for someone who was younger and dumber than they were."

Preferred Industrial Services expanded beyond house painting to replacing floors and roofs and repainting factories in 18 states east of the Mississippi River. His staff grew to 300 people. Annual sales exceeded $25 million. But that growth wasn't without trauma. In 1980, Preferred Industrial Services was losing so much money on a government contract to paint bridges that Craig's accountant advised him to file bankruptcy. Instead, he persuaded his creditors to work with him to keep the company going. "To file bankruptcy wouldn't fit my M.O.," he said.

Only four creditors wouldn't cooperate. He paid them in full and swore never to do business with them again. No one lost a dime, and Preferred Industrial Services came roaring back. However, in 1990, the company was in financial straits again. Craig had to sell stock to outsiders for the first time to save the company. He bought out these investors by 1997. In 1998, Craig divided Preferred Industrial Services into four corporations. He retained minority ownership in three of them and sold what remained.

You never stop learning in business, Craig said. With more than 20 years of business knowledge and expertise, he would expect starting another business to be easier, but said he'd probably discover a new list of learning experiences with any new venture.

8. INVESTIGATE BEFORE BUYING A BUSINESS

Before buying an existing enterprise,
investigate its finances thoroughly.

■ ■ ■

Celia Dorr knew it was time to change careers when she passed out from stress at the big law firm where she had worked for years. A friend of hers was equally in need of a change, so they marched blindly into business ownership. "We thought that if we could buy a secretarial service, it would be easier because we would already have an established customer base," Celia said. "We would have the necessary equipment, and everything would be in place." When Celia and her friend saw an advertisement for a secretarial service in a beach community 40 miles from their homes, they set out to buy it. "We could envision ourselves having wonderful lunches overlooking the ocean, and we'd have a luxurious storefront office," Celia laughed.

The seller was asking $100,000 for the business and equipment, and Celia thought she was driving a hard bargain by offering $85,000. "Thank goodness the business broker had ethics," she said, "because he advised us to make our offer based on the company's books and records."

Celia and her friend hired a business appraiser who first interviewed them about their goals, the services they wanted to offer, their experience, and their target market. Then he interviewed the business seller, inspected the equipment, and reviewed the company's finances. He appraised the business's value at $15,000. The equipment was obsolete and no longer under warranty. It had no contracts to guarantee that a certain amount of work would remain with the company after the sale. The business was not making enough profit to support one business owner, he told them, let alone two. "We were shocked!" Celia said. "We immediately rescinded our offer."

Many inexperienced entrepreneurs believe, as Celia did, that buying an existing business is less risky than starting from scratch. A going concern does have some potential advantages, such as immediate revenue, location, established reputation, contracts, customers, inventory, and equipment. However, many established companies, like old houses, may come with problems. A company's location may be on the decline. Its reputation may be bad. Its equipment may be obsolete, broken, or completely depreciated. And, as Celia discovered, the seller may have an inflated view of the company's worth. While a company with patented products, strong management teams, and a strong competitive advantage can sell for many times its annual profit, a personal service business may sell for an amount equal to or less than a year's profit.

As a prospective buyer, you can do some of the due diligence yourself. First, talk to business neighbors to find out potential problems with the location or the specific company. Also, you can learn a great deal just by hanging around and observing the location and the business at different times during the day. Be cautious about telling anyone you are a prospective buyer, however, because word about a pending sale can harm a business and expose you to a lawsuit by the seller. Unless you understand financial records, hire an expert to examine the books of any company you are thinking about buying. Hire an attorney to review the sales contract.

"Our business appraiser charged us $1,500, and it was the best money I ever spent," Celia said. That appraiser recommended that Celia and her friend start their own secretarial service close to their homes instead of buying one. Sterling Keystroke Services opened in Fullerton, California, in 1989. Celia's partner soon left because of personal problems. Then Celia expanded her secretarial services to include desktop publishing and résumé writing.

Over the years, Celia had several owners offer to sell her their businesses. "Each time, I followed our appraiser's example. I reviewed the books and records, looked at the equipment that was for sale, determined what I was really buying, and, in the end, decided to buy only a portion of one business," she said.

9. KNOW THE RULES

Before launching your business, learn the laws
and local ordinances that affect your enterprise.

■ ■ ■

Janie Williams had worked for tax preparation companies for ten years when she decided to open her own tax and bookkeeping practice in her home in 1993. Imagine her surprise when she went to city hall to get a business license and learned that her municipality prohibits home-based tax preparation businesses. Estimates of the number of home-based businesses range from 18 million to 47 million, depending on who's counting and what is being counted. The technology—personal computers, software, telephone services, and more—that has fostered this growth of home-based businesses has expanded much faster than municipal government's ability and willingness to cope with the phenomenon. Some cities flat out prohibit businesses in the home; most have restrictions that limit the type of work that can be done from home. Even the tax laws are tougher on home-based businesses. But Janie's lesson applies to companies starting out in shopping centers, warehouses, or office buildings, too. Entrepreneurs should investigate zoning laws, lease restrictions, and property association rules before opening their businesses.

Janie said she was fortunate to live in Long Beach, California, which worked with its business owners. Even though she made it clear she would be preparing taxes, the city listed Janie Williams & Associates only as a bookkeeping service, which Long Beach permitted in residential neighborhoods. Janie stressed that home-based business owners should be open and honest with governing entities. It is better to learn the limits in the beginning than to be shut down when an enterprise has contracts and obligations. Janie was careful to abide by another city restriction that limited the number of clients who could visit a home-based business in one day. Many cities don't allow customer traffic, or even employee traffic, to homes, she said. A friend of Janie had two employees working in his home business for two years without incident. Then he remodeled his kitchen. A city inspector checking on the construction noticed and reported the workers, and the city shut down the man's business.

Also, most cities don't allow home-based businesses to have signs. "I wouldn't want one anyway," Janie said. "It would announce to thieves that I had computer equipment on the premises."

Many of the restrictions imposed on businesses in the home are unfair because they don't apply to the same circumstances in which a business isn't present, Janie said. Many cities, for example, prohibit street parking for a business, but have no parking restrictions for houses with five or six adult and teenage drivers. They don't allow a business to have employees, but do allow a homeowner to have a full-time babysitter or housekeeper in the home. They don't allow home businesses to receive deliveries, but wouldn't dream of imposing such a restriction on mail-order shopping junkies. "The laws vary widely across the country and in urban versus rural areas, so each business owner must find out for himself," Janie said. "Also, people who live in condominiums or planned communities have homeowners associations that often have more restrictive rules for home businesses than the cities do."

Many of the restrictions on home-based businesses have sound reasoning behind them. People don't want auto repair shops, toxic chemical plants, or all-night machine shops in quiet, residential neighborhoods. They don't want the streets packed with customers' cars or 12-foot-high neon signs blinking at night. However, most cities don't have enough workers to run around looking for trouble, Janie said. They enforce their home business ordinances on the squeaky-wheel philosophy: if neighbors don't complain, business violations are ignored. "It's important to know the rules, then not be too blatant if you can't abide by all of them," Janie said. "All my neighbors knew what I did. They even came over on street-sweeping day to tell my clients they needed to move their cars."

10. KNOW YOURSELF

The first-time business owner must recognize
and apply previously learned skills and life
experiences to the new venture.

■ ■ ■

Ellen Kruskie's careers as an employee and a business owner couldn't be much further apart. As an employee, she held administrative jobs in medical practices and a biomedical start-up company. When she was laid off—and determined never to allow that to happen again—Ellen started a dog wash service in 1994. Many entrepreneurs don't attempt such a dramatic change in gears. But Ellen didn't concentrate on the differences; she culled her working career for parts and tools that would make Carolina PetSpace in Raleigh, North Carolina, successful.

PetSpace was a do-it-yourself dog wash and accessories boutique specializing in dogs and cats. "While my professional background was in a totally unrelated arena, basic business principles were the same. I don't care if you're running a high-tech company or a dog wash," Ellen said. "Everything you've ever learned or experienced applies."

Before launching her new company, Ellen assessed her background and realized that dealing with people was what she had enjoyed most about working in doctors' offices. "Working one on one with customers at Carolina PetSpace was great," she said. "They didn't just come in here, wash their dogs, and leave. Everyone had a problem. I'm a problem solver. It was not that different from working with patients in a doctor's office."

Being the biomedical start-up's first employee taught Ellen a lot about launching a new company of any type. For the biomedical company, Ellen wrote a business plan that was two-and-a-half inches thick. The plan for PetSpace was 17 pages. She helped find multimillion-dollar funding and 7,000 square feet of industrial space for the biomedical start-up. That experience helped her finance and successfully negotiate a deal for a 2,000-square-foot retail shop for PetSpace. Ellen thoroughly researched the shop's location and talked with everyone she could about the pet industry. "I knew what to look for. I knew the questions to ask," she said. "I just had to reapply the training." Marketing the two businesses was quite different, Ellen added. One focused on attracting venture capital and building scientific credibility for two years before opening its doors. The other sold products, services, and advice directly to consumers.

Ellen's initial plan for PetSpace was to dedicate seven to nine months to research, planning, and construction before opening. "However, the best laid plans can be thwarted by circumstances beyond one's control," she said. "My prep period stretched to nearly 16 months before the doors opened. The preplanning paid off in that while these delays were not desirable, either economically or personally, they were not disastrous either. And the time warp truly tested my resolve." A business owner in any industry must be ready to adjust to the unexpected, Ellen said. But "anticipating and being prepared to accommodate a worst-case scenario for the proposed business eliminates a lot of unpleasant surprises."

When personal experience and skills don't supply an answer, go out and find it, Ellen said. About five months after opening PetSpace, she had the opportunity to buy a complementary business. Her previous employers had never contemplated an expansion, so Ellen had no idea how to evaluate the venture. Ellen sought the assistance of the Service Corps of Retired Executives (SCORE). SCORE's expert advice helped Ellen see that the purchase was unwise. She added the experience to her reservoir of knowledge to be drawn upon in the future.

11. HOBBIES AREN'T BUSINESSES

Without planning, a business owner's need for more
equipment and space can easily consume all the profits.

■ ■ ■

What could be more fun than making chocolate? It was Patricia
Green's favorite hobby. Therefore, in 1980, she and a friend decided to
teach a few candy-making classes and sell supplies. They called their venture The Chocolate Tree. When they leased a small industrial space off the
beaten path, the landlord said they wouldn't last five months. Patricia and
her friend set up a display case housing samples of the candy that students
could learn to make, but customers continually came in and bought the
samples. The owners had to make more samples constantly, and soon they
were out of the hobby business and into manufacturing and retailing.
They didn't realize it, however, because they hadn't thought through what
they were doing. They continued their hobby ways for a long time. In fact,
they hand-dipped pieces of chocolate for two years. "We just went on a
wing and a prayer," Patricia laughed. "Consequently, it took forever to
take money out of the business."

Something always gobbled up the money faster than Patricia could
write herself a paycheck. For example, The Chocolate Tree needed more
space to accommodate the growing number of orders, so Patricia bought
an adjacent building, a former drive-through bank. Later, the company
bought a bigger building, and Patricia and her whole family practically
lived in the factory for months while they added electricity and water.

Also, lack of planning caused mistakes. Patricia once bought a 26-
foot-long machine that was too large to fit in either building she owned.
"Everything we earned we had to put into buildings or equipment. We
should have thought it out more carefully," Patricia said. As a result of her
experience, she wouldn't advocate this growth-without-planning approach
to most start-up businesses. "When you have to pay off debts and reinvest
everything in the business, it takes much too long to make a paycheck,
even a small one," she said.

Many hobbyists who try to turn their crafts into businesses encounter problems. Customers won't pay enough for a finished product to make a business profitable. Large-scale production is difficult to establish. Tasks that were fun on the weekend become grinding chores on a full-time basis. Worst of all, an owner might be so busy with management and marketing that she never gets to participate in the craft she loves.

The Chocolate Tree managed to outgrow its hobby roots without bankrupting the owners. "Turning the tide simply took time—time to get equipment paid off, build inventory, and become known," Patricia said. The Chocolate Tree benefited from serendipity that few small businesses find. The company was located in Beaufort, South Carolina, where the movie *Forrest Gump* was filmed. The shop was not far from the spot where the Tom Hanks character philosophized that life is like a box of chocolates. The tie-in was not lost on tourists—or Hollywood. A team from the Nickelodeon cable channel came to town a few years ago and filmed a segment in The Chocolate Tree. The Chocolate Tree grew to 12 employees who made candy year round. In addition to maintaining the retail store and a mail-order business, the company became a chocolate wholesaler. Patricia still loved teaching how to make chocolate to customers who were content to remain hobbyists.

12. SET YOUR SITES

Spend a little more, if necessary,
to get the right location for your business.

■ ■ ■

Chris McIntyre and Jeffery Brown, coworkers at an international corporation, dreamed of touring Europe on Harley-Davidson motorcycles. But before they could schedule the overseas flight, the dream vacation evolved into the dream business. Chris and Jeff decided to rent Harley-Davidson motorcycles to European tourists in the United States; therefore, they started EagleRider Motorcycle Rental USA in Torrance, California, in 1992. "When we first opened, there was no immediate need for a prime location because we were marketing overseas, and our bookings came through travel agents," Chris said. But the European tourist market proved to be seasonal, so Chris and Jeff started filling the gaps by marketing to Americans.

"Now we needed a higher visibility location," Chris said. "We should have spent more money on rent to secure a more prominent business location." Location can be a make-or-break decision for many types of businesses. Retailers and others like EagleRider that depend on customers finding them need high visibility with adequate parking. Labor-intensive companies, like check processors, need to be near large labor pools. Manufacturers must be located close to highways, rail lines, or ports. Fledgling business owners should evaluate their businesses before even looking for a site. They need to consider their target market—who their customers are and where they're located; whether their customers need to find them; who their competitors are and where they're located; how much space they need; and whether big signs are important.

Chris and Jeff decided EagleRider had to be within ten minutes of international airports in major foreign tourist destinations. The company opened locations in 18 cities including Los Angeles, Denver, Chicago, Las Vegas, and Miami. The Denver location was on the main road between the airport and the downtown. The Chicago operation was open just six months a year because of the city's harsh winters, so it was located in the store of a major seller of Harley-Davidson products and accessories. The alliance benefited both businesses. Although Chris advocated spending more rent to get a prime location, he set limits. The Las Vegas office was a block off the Strip, where the major casinos are located. One block meant the difference between $2-per-square-foot rent and $10 or $15, he said. The new entrepreneur must balance the best possible choice with the business's budget.

All of EagleRider's locations catered mostly to men in their 30s with high disposable incomes. Whether Americans or Europeans, these renters belonged to the passionate following the Harley-Davidson company successfully cultivated for its high-performance motorcycles. They willingly paid a premium to ride their dream bike. But the two customer groups were quite different, Chris said. For Europeans, riding motorcycles was a way of life. Their rentals were longer—ten days to two weeks. For Americans, riding a Harley was a dream fulfillment just for the weekend.

Although EagleRider offered several guided excursions, such as the "Western Legends Ride" tour through California, Nevada, Utah, and Arizona, most Harley-Davidson renters preferred to escape on their own paths and timetables. EagleRider confined its locations to major tourist destinations, which could still fulfill Chris and Jeff's long-term plan to grow the company to the largest motorcycle rental and tour company in the world.

13. HARDER THAN HARD

No one can fully prepare you for how hard it is to run a business.

■ ■ ■

Laurey Masterton grew up in an entrepreneurial family. Her parents owned the Blueberry Hill Inn in Goshen, Vermont, in the early 1960s. Her two sisters—an attorney and a computer consultant—own their own businesses. Laurey owned a commercial interior design firm that decorated showrooms for Hasbro Toys before starting Laurey's Catering and Gourmet-to-Go in Asheville, North Carolina, in 1987. "We all skipped out of the corporate scene," Laurey said. Yet with all that business exposure, "it is really a whole lot harder than I thought it would be. I didn't know catering wasn't going to be the easiest thing. I didn't have a clue, and it's probably a good thing that I didn't."

Of all the challenges that entrepreneurs face, nothing matches in difficulty the everydayness of business ownership. It exists from the moment you wake up until the moment you collapse in exhaustion at the end of the day. It's exhilarating, terrifying, and constant. "I think that the biggest challenge was keeping my spirits up," Laurey said. "Even when I averaged 30 percent growth for five straight years, I still worried. In slower times of the year, I found myself back in the worry mode."

Her background helped get her through the down times. Laurey started her catering business in the kitchen of her second-floor apartment. She had grown up around food, so the business was a return to her roots and a tribute to her mother, who died when Laurey was 12 years old. "I couldn't go back and buy the inn [my parents owned], but I could do my own thing," she said. She learned about business plans, taxes, word-of-mouth advertising, and networking through the Service Corps of Retired Executives. "I created a single-page brochure, went to a local women's networking meeting, and introduced myself as a caterer, even though I did not know *what* I was talking about," Laurey said. She volunteered to cater the group's next meeting. She also placed an ad in the group's newsletter, which brought the first contract, a party for Steelcase, Inc., a maker of office furniture. Many of the group's members remained regular clients and Steelcase continued to be a major account for years.

In the middle of her second year in business, Laurey was diagnosed with ovarian cancer. About the same time as she underwent treatment, she had to take out a large personal loan to pay taxes she hadn't expected. Shaken, but determined and hopeful, she returned to work as soon as she could. As the business grew, Laurey realized she couldn't continue to run the company from her apartment. A private investor, Dana Smith, invested in Laurey's Catering, bringing money, management expertise, emotional support, and down-to-earth advice. They incorporated the company and built a commercial kitchen. Dana asked Laurey to make him dinners that he could pick up on his way home each night. That request led to Gourmet-to-Go, which grew to sell hundreds of gourmet dinners each week. Laurey's Catering expanded to a 2,500-square-foot kitchen and gourmet shop that sold sandwiches and salads. The 12-employee company handled everything from intimate gourmet dinners to company picnics for 2,500 people. "I could have chosen something easier, but I'm glad I took this challenge," Laurey said. "I really feel that the success of this business was something I earned, not something that fell into my lap. You have to be your own worst critic and your own best cheerleader. Every business owner reaches a point when no one will be there telling you 'you can do it; you can do it.' You have to say that yourself."

14. PLAN FOR FAILURE

Failure *can* happen, so a business owner must anticipate
it with worst-case scenarios when planning.

■ ■ ■

In 1982, Gerald Brong resigned his professorship at Washington State University to open Community Computer Centers, a value-added reseller of Kaypro computers. Within two years, the university was his major competition and dominated the market. As a nonprofit entity exempt from certain business and income taxes, the University could beat Gerald's prices. Gerald put too much money into inventory for a brand that was a loser in the computer wars. His business went bankrupt.

In the bright-eyed days before opening their ventures, too few business owners allow themselves to think about the possibility of failure. Gerald said he should have built into his vision an escape plan in case something went wrong. With a worst-case scenario in hand, Gerald could have taken businesslike action to close the company before every dime of his savings and retirement funds were gone. Although the federal bankruptcy system is designed to give individuals and business owners a fresh start, don't let anyone tell you bankruptcy is the easy way out. Reestablishing credit and savings can take years. After filing for bankruptcy, Gerald and his wife, Marlene, had no assets, credit cards, or health insurance. They owed back taxes that were not discharged in the bankruptcy, plus 24 percent penalties and interest on those taxes. Gerald couldn't get his old teaching job back because his company had competed with the university's venture. "We lost friends. They were embarrassed. They didn't want to hear about my failure," Gerald said.

The Brong family rebuilt its business one brick at a time. "Having hit the bottom of the barrel and bounced around in the slop, there were only two things to do: Either drown in the slop or get out of the barrel," Gerald said. "Drowning didn't seem like an acceptable option." The Brongs began by writing a business plan for their new business, which they named GMB Partnership. Gerald concentrated on writing, speaking, consulting, and training. One of his rules for this venture was to do nothing that required any up-front cash or inventory. For example, if a client hired Gerald to assemble a computer system, the client bought the equipment first.

"In finding self-employment following failure, I developed business activities that conserved cash, leveraged capital, and used intangible assets to generate positive cash flow," Gerald said. "I sold intellect, ideas, and available human time." The Brongs decided to return to the Kittitas Valley in Washington State, where they married. "There was a good university library here," Gerald said. Plus, "The rural community didn't judge people on their trappings." That was helpful when the Brongs didn't have many trappings. Vacations consisted of picnics in the backyard of their rented house. For entertainment, the family attended $3 concerts at the nearby university. After the bankruptcy, Gerald couldn't even rent a car when he went on business trips because he didn't have a credit card. However, he had kept his membership in Rotary International, and a fellow member, a bank manager, eventually cosigned for a credit card. "Though there was frequently the 'I give up' response," he said, "It became obvious that giving up wasn't as much fun as survival."

15. GET OFF THE DIME

Eventually, you have to quit planning and start the business.

■ ■ ■

After years in sales and training for international corporations, Larry Dybis launched his own business. Actually, he was given a shove. He did such a good job setting up one company's marketing program, the boss decided he didn't need anyone to run it. Larry was out of a job. "I had been building up other companies for years," Larry said. "I decided, this time I would do it for myself." So, in 1995, Larry began People Dynamics in Western Springs, Illinois, a firm dedicated to strategic planning, training, and career coaching.

In a way, Larry was doing what he saw so many of his clients do: procrastinating. Procrastination is a symptom of uncertainty and fear. The would-be business owner spends excessive amounts of time finding an office, looking for furniture, and investigating multiple phone lines. "I should have spent less time getting ready," Larry said. "Not that a person should not know what to do and how to do it, but overpreparing with excessive focus on 'I must know more, practice more, organize more' only delays your natural ramp-up time." A new business requires a year or two to become established, pay its dues, and gain recognition among potential clients, he said. "Delaying this for any reason just makes the process more difficult and harder to endure."

One simple aid is to set a deadline for starting the business and stick to it, even if you haven't completed every task on your to-do list. Another is to slice off a small piece of the whole project and complete it. Or try the sneak attack. Do a task immediately before your mind has time to resist. Force yourself to put the most unpleasant task first. Once that's done, many of the fun parts of business start-up will flow.

Larry said he later recognized these delaying tactics in many of his clients who wanted to start professional speaking or seminar practices. "They didn't want to be humiliated by delivering less than their best quality or value that they promised, so they worked endlessly on their businesses," he said. "I told them they had a tremendous amount of potential, but they must work to make sure it wasn't permanent potential." Larry urged these clients to go out and give speeches for free. They didn't have to have three-day seminars in hand to do that, he said. "Give it away. That's how you establish connections and reputation; then build on it," he advised. "You need a feedback system to keep going. When you see the lightbulbs go on while you're speaking, and people come up afterward and thank you, that validates your work."

Many entrepreneurs encounter resistance to their prices when trying to get their first clients. Larry suggested charging on an escalating scale. Charge your standard price, say $1,000, and give the client a $500 gift certificate. The understanding is that if the client recognizes the value of your work, the next project or program will cost $750, then $900, and finally your $1,000 standard fee. "You're ramping yourself up, not just giving it away," Larry explained. "But do this only with someone who could become a good client. I had a friend who described it this way: He said he was willing to polish a diamond in the rough, but he didn't polish bricks. Some people just aren't worth this approach."

Regardless of preparation and planning, the final plunge into business ownership requires commitment, Larry said. "Don't tell yourself you're going to give it a year and see if it works out. Go after it completely, and success becomes a matter of time."

PART 2

EARLY DECISIONS

■ ■ ■

The most frightening period for the new entrepreneur is not the pre-start-up phase. That's fantasy time. The reality of small-business ownership sets in after you have made the commitment. The early decisions, once you're sailing the entrepreneurial seas, set the course.

New business owners tend to ignore the future consequences of their actions. Perhaps the most important task during the early days is to tune your attitude. Expect a positive outcome. Thicken your skin. Avoid reading evil motives into every adverse occurrence. Adopt a posture of consistent persistence.

Like most new business owners, you might want to grab every customer who crosses your path, fearful another might never come along. Later, you will develop confidence that your products or services really do have value in the marketplace. Then you will weed out the losers, the late payers, and the complainers. Similarly, you might begin by offering too many products and services, again fearful that you won't make a living if you focus too sharply. Later, your confidence will allow you to dump the unprofitable lines. Lo and behold, you'll be even more profitable. You wouldn't have believed it at first.

16.

TAKE THE BUSINESS SERIOUSLY

Low expectations and half-hearted efforts will
drag down even a good business concept.

■ ■ ■

When Doris Christopher's second daughter started school in 1980, she wanted to find work that was rewarding yet allowed her flexibility to put family first. She considered what she might be able to do with her education and experience as a home economist. Doris realized that her friends marveled at her kitchen gadgets that helped turn out wonderful meals and saved time as well. Selling these products just might be a business, but retail wouldn't give her the flexibility she wanted, so Doris decided to try selling them directly to customers through what she called kitchen shows. She borrowed $3,000 on a life insurance policy to buy her first inventory. As she arrived at a friend's home for her first event, she thought, "This is the stupidest thing I've ever done." By the time she went home, having sold $175 worth of products and booked four more shows, she had changed her mind and thought this idea could be her calling. The Pampered Chef was born in the basement of her River Forest, Illinois, home.

Doris never thought of The Pampered Chef as a lark that she would abandon on a whim. "Even though it was a small venture, I realized I must take the business seriously," Doris said. "In my heart of hearts I hoped it would grow and be successful." Doris started with about 30 items she couldn't do without in her kitchen. She ordered by the dozen and paid cash because she didn't have a line of credit. By the end of the first year, she had sales of $50,000 and 12 independent consultants doing kitchen shows just as Doris did. The venture grew quickly, demanding more time and business expertise. Much of her management style was common sense and instinct. Doris knew her products and how to make presentations, but she didn't know about direct selling, distribution, or finance. So she learned as she went. Fortunately, her husband, Jay, had marketing and business expertise. Doris joined the Direct Selling Association. She switched from delivering products to customers in person to using UPS. After the initial loan, she grew The Pampered Chef without debt into the world's largest direct seller of high-quality kitchen tools and accessories. It grew by 2003 to sales of $740 million, 1,000 coworkers, and 71,000 independent consultants who were running their own businesses giving kitchen shows to sell more than 200 products, most of which were exclusive to The Pampered Chef. Although Doris sold the company to Berkshire Hathaway in 2002, she remained chairman, active in daily operations.

"The starting point of any business should be whether you really love it. If you love what you're doing, you don't mind working hard; if you hate it, that's impossible," Doris said. Initially, she was able to set her own hours, remain flexible for family activities, and insist on family mealtime. As The Pampered Chef grew, a multitude of demands made Doris work even harder. "I was heavily devoted to the business and put in many hours. I was surprised at my willingness to do that. What I was doing was so well received; it was a success on a lot of levels. Personally, it allowed me to work in an area I felt was satisfying. Ultimately, it was financially successful. It was exhilarating, so that it gave me energy." Doris mentored other women entrepreneurs and continually encouraged The Pampered Chef consultants who essentially were running their own businesses. She urged them to take their businesses seriously in order to earn personal satisfaction along with money.

17. FIND YOUR NICHE

It is more profitable to establish yourself as the
expert in a narrow, well-defined field than to
try to know a little about everything.

■ ■ ■

After graduating from law school, Marla Merhab Robinson was in-house counsel for a manufacturing and real estate company. She was expected to know a little about any legal issue that came up. But then she joined an independent law firm in Santa Ana, California. "All of us had strong corporate law backgrounds," she said, "but all the other lawyers had another area of practice at which they were particularly strong. There was an estate planner, a real estate guru, a securities expert, and a tax expert."

Marla needed her own area of expertise that didn't overlap the specialties of all the other attorneys in her law firm. She didn't expect it to become her primary practice, just a way to differentiate herself from other attorneys. One day she received a continuing education brochure from the state bar association about why every company should have an employee handbook. The firm's managing partner allowed Marla to write all existing clients and offer to review their existing handbook of company policies for free. If any work resulted from her recommendations, she charged her regular rate. "That's how I learned employment law."

Attorneys aren't the only businesspeople who benefit from identifying one area of expertise in which to distinguish themselves. Even entrepreneurs who have a product or service that everyone can use—say bookkeeping or a cleaning service—save time and energy by focusing on one type of customer or one geographic location. They can provide high quality at a premium price for being the best in their field. A jack-of-all-trades rarely can.

The employment law specialty was helpful when Marla opened her own law office in order to have more control over her time and greater flexibility with her children. "Lawyers are ethically prohibited from accepting jobs that we don't feel we can do competently," she said. Fortunately, employment legal issues were increasingly important in U.S. business and kept her busy. She spent half her time on employment law and half on non-litigation business issues. "I didn't aspire to be the owner, so it was one of the most difficult things I ever did," she said, "but one of the best. It allowed me to do just what I wanted."

Employment law also gave her other revenue generators, such as teaching seminars on avoiding sexual harassment in the workplace, effective hiring and firing, and proper employment documentation. Her initial employee handbook review was also a marketing tool. She modified it to be a complete employment audit for a flat fee. Some took only a week; others six months. But the review was her "loss leader," introducing her employment law competence to new clients. "This made me not just an expert on the law, but an expert on them," she said. "I could tell immediately, from my review, which companies were going to have employee problems."

18. THE SUPPORT SYSTEM IS GONE

New business owners who are corporate refugees don't realize
how much they relied on their old workplaces for validation,
services, interaction, and emotional support.

■ ■ ■

Tracey Campbell was a financial journalist and market prognostica-
tor for a business services giant. Her husband dreamed of owning his own
business but lacked the "swing from the chandelier and leap" personality,
as Tracey phrased it. So, in 1995, she leaped instead, creating 1-888-Inn-
Seek, a 24-hour telephone and Internet service set up to search for bed-
and-breakfast inns throughout the United States.

If you're one of those corporate dwellers whose company is heartless,
whose boss is a jerk, whose coworkers are strangers, and whose job is joy-
less, think twice about chucking it all for your own business, Tracey said.
"I took for granted the infrastructure built into my job. The office supply
closet was always stocked. Information Services was always there to fix
my computer."

Tracey operated 1-888-Inn-Seek from a Danbury, Connecticut, farm-
house that was almost three centuries old, give or take a few decades. If
Tracey ran out of envelopes, she drove to the store. If her computer broke
down, she spent hours on the telephone, holding for the manufacturer's
technical support line, or she spent the afternoon traveling back and forth
to the nearest computer store. She rebuilt her computer server twice. Once,
all three hard drives crashed simultaneously. When a potential client asked
for a brochure for 1-888-Inn-Seek, she had to create her own. When she
ordered 10,000 tent business cards, she had to fold them herself.

The psychological side is equally important, Tracey said. "There is
something about getting a paycheck that validates what you do. You write
a memo, and it goes someplace, and people read it. I used to do a lot of television and radio appearances, so I got some fan mail. "I've never thought
of myself as an egomaniac, so I never thought I would miss all that."

To combat her isolation and lack of experience, Tracey started a Web
Girls chapter, which provided support for women learning computers and

technology. To avoid bogging down in a sea of menial tasks sucking away her limited time, she found a nearby sheltered workshop that charged just $10 for every thousand business cards folded and tied with ribbon into bundles of ten. The computers would always be a challenge, but Tracey learned to do some of her own programming and local networking.

1-888-Inn-Seek originally was going to fax information back to callers, but Tracey couldn't find satisfactory software. Instead, callers could search the database of inns by using a Touch-Tone phone. The same information could be searched many ways on the Web site, which had thousands of visitors a day. Visitors could search by location, amenities, or special events. They could find inns that allow pets. They could search for an inn near a friend's home by entering the friend's telephone number. Some innkeepers and event planners paid to add descriptions of their offerings to the phone service and Web site. As Tracey discovered more sources of help and information, learned to handle tasks once left to corporate assistants, and expanded marketing avenues, her memories of corporate support dimmed. But she still couldn't find anyone to read her memos.

19. THE VALUE OF A GOOD NAME

You will fight an uphill battle if your company name
isn't unique and easy for customers to remember.

■ ■ ■

At first glance NoUVIR seems like a nonsensical name, but it's worth more than gold to Ruth Ellen Miller, president of NoUVIR Research in Seaford, Delaware. When she and her scientist father Jack V. Miller started the company in 1990, they knew they needed a unique, easily remembered name that could be trademarked. Although Ruth Ellen thought NoUVIR was a great name for her company from the beginning, she also knew it would take time to establish because it was not a word. The company had to teach people how to pronounce the name, which made it harder to establish initially but also made it a strong trademark.

"A great name is one of the best marketing tools you can have, and it will pick up speed on its own as it really supports word-of-mouth advertising," Ruth Ellen said. "But you have to be able to protect it because big competitors with more money will steal anything you don't legally nail down."

But what did NoUVIR mean? It didn't make sense unless you knew that the company manufactured fiber optic lighting that had no ultraviolet (called UV in the lighting industry) and no infrared radiation (IR). So, no UV or IR. This type of lighting was vital in museums, such as the Smithsonian Institution in Washington, D.C., where documents like the Declaration of Independence were being destroyed by regular light. In fact, NoUVIR was founded because of Ruth Ellen's desire to protect historically important paintings and documents from cracking and fading because of exposure to sunlight. Jack agreed to participate if his daughter would run the company. They spent more than four years on research and development before putting any product on the market. The company expanded to make a whole range of fiber optic lights from floodlights to luminaires with a beam the size of a penny to candle-like fiber optic lights.

NoUVIR was a name instantly understood by museum curators, restaurateurs with extensive wine cellars, and others responsible for protecting and preserving important, light-sensitive objects. Customers included the Library of Congress, Major League Baseball Hall of Fame, and, of course, the Smithsonian Institution.

"You can do all the marketing in the world, and if your name is not unique and cannot be remembered by your customer, you will always be fighting an uphill battle," Ruth Ellen said. "What was dumb luck was how important the name became when we set up our Web site. I had a competitor that if you used their name with www and followed by .com you get a totally different company. That hurt them."

The unique name was also useful in large corporate databases. Customers' accounting departments and government agencies never confused NoUVIR with any other company, Ruth Ellen said.

When trademarking the name, Ruth Ellen also trademarked "no IR." That was helpful when a huge corporation started advertising its line of fiber optics as "no IR."

"I suspect a lawyer yelled at someone in that company because the ads stopped," she said. "But the idea that a large company copied that phrase was startling. There were dozens of other ways to say light is heatless. Everyone who read the ad and knew about NoUVIR thought about us."

20. THE VALUE OF BEING FIRST

Duplicating what someone already provides in a niche market is a loser's formula. Find your own specialty.

■ ■ ■

Bud Blackburn was a farmer and jack-of-all-trades when his Uncle Ray, a land surveyor, came to him with an idea. In the 1940s, surveyors used heavy lath sticks to mark their work. Ray thought a lighter weight flag would be more efficient. Bud spent about four years developing, in his spare time, a machine to produce the flags, and in 1953 he opened Blackburn Manufacturing with his father and uncle on the family farm south of Royal, Nebraska.

It would have been futile for the Blackburns to copy the lath sticks already in use, said Bud's son, Jim, president of the company since 1980. To survive and thrive, a small company must be first and different. "Me-too-ism" is a killer. "I believe our company's success can be attributed to being the first company to introduce this niche product," Jim said. Blackburn Manufacturing's first customers were soil and water conservation districts that needed markers for laying out terraces that prevent erosion. The Blackburns refused to go into debt to start their little venture. Still, demand grew steadily. After four years, the company was selling so many flags that Bud sold the farm and went into flag making full time.

Jim, who grew up in the business, worked on the company's first million-flag order when he was a boy. After a stint in the Navy, Jim joined the company full time in 1973. At the same time, Bill Lawson became a partner, bringing with him a process of silk screening names and labels onto the flags. This process opened the specialty product to a new market, utility companies. Blackburn Manufacturing adapted the utilities' color coding, such as red flags to mark electrical lines and green flags for sewer pipes. The flags certainly were not glamorous, but they were so useful and inexpensive that many industries wanted them.

"Considering the business environment in the 1950s and 1960s, I believe the slow and steady growth of the business combined with zero indebtedness were primary factors in our business success. It was especially beneficial in the 1980s, with interest rates and inflation in the double digits."

Blackburn Manufacturing exploited its competitive advantage in the marking-flag market to the fullest. When you see small plastic flags used at construction sites, in landscaping projects and nurseries, or by utilities, chances are Blackburn Manufacturing made those flags. Without leaving the niche it dominates, the company added accessory products, such as tape, marking paint, and different types of staffs on which to hang the flags. "We have always been a very self-sufficient company in that we build our own flag machines from scratch and our own buildings as they have become necessary for expansion," said Jim.

The 57-employee company, which moved to Neligh, Nebraska, also remained a family operation. Jim's brother, Bob, managed one of two factories. His brother-in-law was sales manager. Also, Jim's daughter and Bob's son were both active in the business.

Just because Blackburn Manufacturing was first, didn't mean it could depend on maintaining its leadership without effort. The company kept profit margins low enough to discourage big companies from trying to compete. Plain four-inch by five-inch flags sold for less than four cents apiece in orders of more than 25,000. Obviously, volume was an important factor in Blackburn Manufacturing's success. The company sold 168 million marking flags each year and boasted 25,000 customers worldwide. "I keep looking over my shoulder expecting someone to invent a better mouse trap, make a better flag," Jim said. "But it's such a niche product, and we have always been very customer-oriented."

21. PAY ATTENTION TO YOU

Don't let the hard work of starting and building a business destroy your health.

■ ■ ■

When Ann Reizer and Marshall Hovivian started Martin Integrated Systems in Orange, California, in 1989, energy and good health were their most abundant assets, although they appeared nowhere on the balance sheet. The pair had worked together at a general contracting company and decided to create their own specialty subcontracting firm to install ceilings in commercial buildings. Marshall had the business contacts and construction expertise. Ann, with MBA and a certified public accounting designation, handled the tasks of estimating job costs and keeping the books.

Instead of aiming to be the low bidder, Martin Integrated emphasized high quality and service. That was a unique philosophy in the construction industry, Ann said. It required plenty of hands-on work in setting up the management systems and training workers to follow the high-service style. "We had to be there to put our imprint on every procedure, every job," she said. "We were feeling our way along. When a client called up and said, 'I need it tomorrow,' we had to be able to say yes."

They worked 14-hour days, six days a week.

Most of her life Ann had just two colds a year, one each spring and fall, with rare bouts of the flu or bronchitis thrown in. Once she became a business owner she worked through minor illnesses. If she got tired, she drank a Coke. "I'm one of those people who thinks sleeping is a waste of time," Ann said. "But you only have so much reserve you can draw on. Then every cold turns into bronchitis; every bronchitis turns into asthma."

In 1995, Ann had a stroke.

In hindsight, warning signs were plentiful. She had been in two car accidents, so she didn't sleep well because of continual pain. A personal relationship ended. Those factors wore down her immune system, Ann said, and she got bronchitis that antibiotics couldn't stop. She had four asthma attacks that sent her to the emergency room. Twice she was hospitalized. "I basically ignored all of it," Ann said. Yet her unrelenting work schedule combined with poor diet and little exercise contributed to her deteriorating health, which culminated in the stroke. How else could she explain it? She had low cholesterol and no evidence of heart problems. Following the stroke Ann had occasional seizures. The damage to her lungs was permanent. Ann used to go on vacations where she hiked eight miles without breathing hard. After the stroke she couldn't walk on a treadmill without taking a breathing treatment first. Fatigue is a constant companion. After three hours of activity, she needs a nap.

Ann said she and Marshall should have trained others so the company wasn't so dependent on their constant presence. After the management and financial systems were in place, they could have done that, but they didn't change gears. Marshall was able to keep Martin Integrated going after Ann's stroke by working even harder. His wife, Cindy, a company officer, also put in long hours, and the rest of the staff scrambled to learn and take on the work Ann had done. Fortunately for Ann, Martin Integrated had bought disability insurance for the two partners just a year before her stroke. It replaced her salary, so she didn't have financial worries along with the nagging health concerns. "Most start-ups don't buy disability insurance because it's tremendously expensive, especially for women," Ann said.

"Would I have escaped all the health problems if I had taken better care of myself? It's too iffy to say," according to Ann. "But definitely I *can* say that if you work 14, 18 hours a day long enough, you will ruin your health."

22.   DON'T TAKE IT PERSONALLY

In business, rejection isn't personal.
Make enough calls, and eventually you will get jobs.

■ ■ ■

Leticia Herrera got into the cleaning business to keep a promise to a friend. The friend had done her a favor and in return asked for the name of a Hispanic-owned janitorial service. Leticia's referral backed out of the job at the last minute, so she recruited her mother and aunt—the best cleaners she knew—and did the job herself. "I never even cleaned my own house," she said. "I didn't think of getting paid; I just had to keep my word." When the check arrived a month later, Leticia couldn't even remember what she had called her "company." But she realized that the $1,200 payment minus her expenses was more than she made in two weeks at her regular job.

So Extra Clean, Inc. (now called ECI), became an official business in Chicago, Illinois, in 1989. Its seemingly easy beginning quickly gave way to the harsh realities of trying to win cleaning contracts without a corporate history, reputation, or savings account. Perseverance was Leticia's only nourishment in a steady diet of rejection by potential customers. It toughened her skin and her resolve. "In small business, we get too personal. My business is my baby. That's me. That's my reputation," Leticia said. "But it's not personal." Customers are looking for solutions for themselves. They are not trying to harm or help fledgling companies. To win business, entrepreneurs need to offer those solutions. And they need to offer them as many times as it takes to find a yes.

Leticia learned that if she made enough sales calls, eventually someone would throw a little work her way. Sometimes it took a hundred calls. Then she learned that if she did a good job, more work would follow. "When I first started, I did anything," she said. "They never give you the easy stuff. They give you whatever no one else could do, expecting you to fail like everyone else."

Her willingness to tackle the most difficult cleaning tasks led ECI to a lucrative niche that became the main focus of the company: stone cleaning and restoration. During the early 1990s, the janitorial industry was changing. Small companies like ECI had increasing difficulty competing with large corporations for routine maintenance contracts. ECI almost went bankrupt. Leticia asked one client for additional work, and he said other cleaning companies had been unable to clean the terrazzo in his building. Leticia didn't know how to clean it either, but she loved art and architecture, so she turned to European experts to learn how to clean marble and other stone. "We were like bulldogs," she said. "Four or five other companies had failed. I wasn't about to."

Success on that project led to other unusual and emergency cleaning projects. That's when Leticia decided to ease out of routine maintenance to concentrate on stone cleaning and restoration, which have higher profit margins. The new focus led to projects for Carrara Marble & Mosaic Co., the Chicago Museum of Contemporary Art, the Democratic National Convention, the Field Museum, and hundreds more needing the specialty cleaning and restoration service. Cleaning and restoring stone and metal is labor intensive, so most of ECI's competitors didn't want to do it. "I used European products, but in Italy, they took a year to clean something. Can you imagine me taking a year for one of my clients?" said Leticia, who loved the specialty's artistic aspect. Leticia's persistence in seeking contracts grew ECI to 90 employees and more than $2 million in annual revenues. "Success is a daily thing," she said. "Even if I have bad days, I will succeed if I don't give up. Every failure I have had has been followed by a greater blessing."

23. LEASING ISSUES

While a retail store needs a good location, the lease may
actually be more important for survival and success.

■ ■ ■

While Kelly Comarda was a baseball pitcher for Tulane University in New Orleans, Louisiana, in 2003, it bothered him that most local retailers only carried licensed sports clothing and other products for Louisiana State University. As a business major, Kelly decided to do more about this hole in the market than just talk about it. "We can make money selling the clothes of the smaller schools," he said. So he decided to open a store called Home Teams to sell T-shirts, caps, jackets, and other gear for Tulane, Southern University, Nicholls State University, and other Louisiana college and professional teams. The store was also a sales outlet for Kelly's exclusive casual clothing line called Muhfuka.

The traditional adage for retailers is that success depends on three factors: location, location, location. Kelly quickly discovered that finding good retail space in the first place was tough. He first considered a strip shopping center, but after researching the market he chose an enclosed shopping center, Clearview Mall in Metairie, Louisiana, near New Orleans because it was on the busiest intersection in the state.

The less obvious retail adage is that an unfavorable lease can kill a new shop. New retailers must be mindful that a standard lease offered by the landlord is always one-sided in favor of the lessor, and it's harder to negotiate terms with a popular center than a poor location. Commercial leases are usually written in legalese. A word change here or there can have a major financial effect on earnings for years. "The lease specified every single thing you could and couldn't sell," Kelly said. "We were thinking about adding athletic shoes and we had to go back and get permission. They insisted you go to arbitration rather than court if there was a legal dispute and also tried to lock you into the space for as long as possible, which was hard on a new business."

Many leases require tenants to pay their own janitorial service, landscape maintenance, common area maintenance, and more. These fees can really add up, especially if a new retailer hasn't anticipated them. "There were all kinds of hidden costs," Kelly said. "They picked up your trash and charged you $60 a month. The lease had 'miscellaneous expense;' I made them spell out everything that included. I wanted to know where the money went." Tenants need to watch for clauses in the lease that seem to have nothing to do with money but nevertheless are extremely valuable. One common example is the nondisturbance clause. Tenants that don't have such a clause can be forced to leave or sign a new, more expensive lease, if the shopping center is sold.

Home Teams opened right before the 2003 football season. The mall had been rejuvenated with national retail chains and a 12-screen movie theater but was still rebuilding traffic from its former image and the 2001 recession. Home Teams got a good location across from the food court and movie theaters' box office. Kelly and other shop owners immediately began pushing the mall management to do more advertising and marketing to boost foot traffic even more.

Kelly discovered another factor about location. It could greatly change a business model. "Our plan changed so much since we opened," he said. "We decided that men don't shop in malls all that often, and we would be better suited to cater to women and especially children." He also discovered that despite his Tulane ties, as a businessman he couldn't ignore LSU, especially after the football team won the Sugar Bowl and the Bowl Championship Series national championship in 2004. But then, that's business.

24.

A DAMAGING ASSOCIATION

Check out your location and building carefully.
You can't imagine the damage to your company
if the building is poorly maintained or half-empty.

■ ■ ■

When Sharon Kelly started a company to publish how-to books for the spa industry, she couldn't find an office in downtown Anchorage, Alaska, in which she could share secretarial and office services. Therefore, she decided to open her own executive office suite. She looked for space for more than four years. Office building owners wanted three years' rent in advance to take a chance on both an unproven concept and someone who had no experience in the endeavor. Finally, she was able to rent 3,000 square feet in an empty office building, and in 1992 Sharon opened Mid-town Executive Office Suite. "An empty building was a difficult location for a start-up business," she said. "Couple this with a building that wasn't kept clean, and it was devastating. If you were on the second floor, as I was, you would have no control over the first impression people had of your business. Even if your suite was high class and the staff extremely competent, clients still judged you by the mess outside the door.

Location and appearance are important to many types of businesses. Sharon recommended that new entrepreneurs visit a site they're thinking about leasing at different times of day both on weekdays and on the weekend. If she had visited the office building at night, she would have noticed that it had no outside signs or lights. It was virtually invisible. Sharon also recommended talking to the building's janitors and tenants to learn how well a building and its grounds are maintained. Other factors can be important in evaluating commercial space. A company might want street-level access, ample free parking, or nearby restaurants, for example. It was important to Sharon to have her executive suite in a top-quality office building.

She avoided moving out of the old location for several years because she had invested her life savings, $30,000, in tenant improvements in the suite. However, when she lost her last client in December 1996, she started looking elsewhere. In October 1997, Sharon moved Midtown Executive Office Suite to another building. Because she had a track record in the executive suite industry, Sharon was able to persuade another landlord to accept her business. However, she applied the lessons she learned from her first office search. She talked with the cleaning service and tenants, who told her the new space was immaculately maintained and any problems were repaired promptly. She negotiated an outside sign for her company. She visited at night to make sure passersby could see the building. She also insisted on a clause that no interior construction for tenant build-outs would disrupt her business during working hours. Sharon said entrepreneurs should check a building owner's background for lawsuits or unpaid taxes. "This one entity can make or break your business," she said. "Make sure it is in tune with you and your company."

Each location has a personality that affects your business. In the first location, Sharon received secretarial work from some tenants, but the second building housed larger tenants that had their own secretaries. However, it was across the street from a business hotel, whose residents brought her much more walk-in business than she used to have. In both locations, her executive suites attracted traveling salespeople, large corporations looking for branch offices, and home-based entrepreneurs in need of commercial addresses and meeting space. Eventually, Anchorage attracted more executive suites, but Sharon didn't consider them to be competition. "I saw them as allies. If they were full, they referred people to me, and if my suite wasn't right for [a prospective tenant], I referred him to one of the other executive suites."

25. BALANCE NICHE WITH DIVERSITY

Although businesses should specialize, they need
enough diversity to avoid economic downturns
that hit one industry or region.

■ ■ ■

The entrepreneurial bug bit Terry Anderson after he had worked for others as a design engineer, buyer, and salesperson for the better part of the 1960s and 1970s. He and his wife, Nancy, started Omni Tech, a manufacturer's representative firm, in their Pewaukee, Wisconsin, home in 1978. The firm sold fabricated metal products. It grew rapidly to $7.5 million in sales, with 80 percent of the business coming from the agriculture and heavy equipment industries. In 1981 and 1982, both industries hit a recession. Omni Tech's business declined 70 percent in 18 months. A $4 million contract with Caterpillar Tractor plummeted to $50,000, and a $1.5 million contract with International Harvester plunged to $75,000.

"I wasn't street savvy about running a business," Terry said. If he had been, he would have avoided concentrating too much on two major accounts with just one type of product. To survive in business, Terry reduced the company back to its core and returned to making his own sales calls again. But for long-term success, Terry decided on a different strategy. "It was imperative that Omni Tech never again put all its eggs in one basket, but have several separate businesses," he said. "If one business cycle was down, another part would be up." The key was to diversify while still specializing, a neat trick that many entrepreneurs can't pull off in a crisis mode. To his credit, Terry didn't give in to the temptation to try to sell all products to everyone. Instead, he developed two parallel specialty divisions that matched his engineering and sales background.

One part of the business would design and make specialized sheet metal products for organizations that lacked in-house capabilities to build their own. Drawing on his engineering background, Terry designed and patented an enclosure for Apple IIe computers for the Milwaukee, Wisconsin, public schools. The fixtures eliminated tampering and secured the computers to desktops to avoid theft. Soon Omni Tech was selling these units to schools throughout the country. A short time later, to complete Terry's diversified specialty strategy, Omni Tech started building custom IBM-compatible computers for customers' specific needs.

The diversified specialty strategy was a wise one, Terry said. When the price of Apple IIe computers declined from $2,100 to $600, schools no longer felt the need to protect the equipment with costly security enclosures. Instead of suffering another financial tailspin, Omni Tech expanded its computer division while its design technology division developed other products. The designers came up with a modular, wall-mounted enclosure for computers at 2,200 Kentucky Fried Chicken fast-food restaurants. Later they created computer shelves for the back offices in 7-Eleven convenience stores owned by Southland Corp. For its part, the computer division didn't try to sell to the mass market, Terry said. "We sold personal computers to a targeted list of large corporations that we invited to become customers of ours in a win-win situation."

Omni Tech's sales grew from $1.2 million in 1989 to $105 million eight years later. The company moved into an 18,000-square-foot building in 1993 and added an 11,000-square-foot office in 1995. The product mix helped Omni Tech secure financing its growth. One side was capital intensive with high inventory and receivables, while the other required little upfront capital. However, the growth didn't proceed as smoothly as it sounds. "It took us ten years to find the right path," Terry said, "but I didn't know what I didn't know."

26. INVESTMENTS THAT DIFFERENTIATE

Immediate investment in technology can set a company apart
and make it more difficult for competitors to enter the market.

■ ■ ■

In 1984, Cameron James and Ken Mills were coworkers at an Ohio video production company when they asked each other a simple question: Was corporate demand for video likely to grow in Columbus, Ohio? Of course. So the pair invested several thousand dollars to form Mills/James Productions. They rented the essential equipment and started making corporate videos for local businesses. Cameron and Ken worked as independent producers, contracting for the services needed on each project.

Mills/James rented the equipment it needed because, at that time, a broadcast-quality editing suite cost $2 million. That approach put Mills/James at the mercy of the companies that owned the equipment. Equipment availability limited the projects the company could go after. The obvious problem for start-ups is obtaining the cash to acquire the technology. Loans are difficult to come by. Investors want higher profit margins than many industries command. The entrepreneurs must take steps that will build barriers to stymie competition from entering the market. Cameron admitted he wasn't much of a risk taker. Surprised? Don't be. Many people who start businesses and grow them into major successes don't consider themselves speculators, just seizers of opportunity.

In 1988, Mills/James was given the opportunity to manage the video production division for Discovery Systems. Mills/James not only shared the profits, but gained access to $2 million in equipment. The company added postproduction and graphics services to its offerings. Its staff more than doubled. "That catapulted us to great growth and rapid expansion," Cameron said. Mills/James derived a double benefit from owning the high-tech equipment required in its industry. Potential competitors had to spend more money to enter the market, and possessing equipment that few others had allowed Mills/James to charge more for its services. "In hindsight, I would have invested in technology immediately, although it would have required greater risk and careful planning," Cameron said.

Once Mills/James started reaping the benefits of owning its technology, it continued to make the investments that separated it from the competition. In 1990, the company built its own 25,000-square-foot production facility rather than convert an existing building, which is the more common approach. Five years later, the company added 22,000 square feet of space. Few production facilities offered the range of film, videoconferencing, special events, radio, television, CD-ROM, and Internet services that Mills/James could provide under one roof, Cameron said. The company's clients ranged from corporations to government agencies. Instead of being the tenant, the company rented its equipment and production facilities to advertising agencies and others. In 1997, Mills/James was the sixteenth largest contract production company in the United States, with 130 employees and annual revenue of $15 million.

While Ohio isn't recognized as the heartland of the video industry, it had a great influence on Mills/James's development into a one-stop source for media and special events, Cameron said. "We had a fraction of the overhead in Columbus versus the West Coast or New York," he explained. "There are more boutique [limited-service] companies on the two coasts." However, the Internet changed the level of competition in the industry. A video company could put libraries of clients' videos on the Internet, and executives could view them on personal computers at their desks anywhere in the world. That opened new markets to Mills/James, but also opened its market strongholds to international companies. "We work in a business that is changing at the speed of light," Cameron said. "It is change brought about by changing marketplaces, changing technologies, and changing customer demands. We must constantly reevaluate how we do things. What was good enough yesterday might not be good enough tomorrow. Change is not always easy, but it is essential. If you're not hurting, you're probably not growing."

27. THE RIGHT STUFF

Don't settle for cheaper equipment that doesn't meet
your company needs in order to save money.
The costs will be greater in the long run.

■ ■ ■

In 1977, the Alaska Transportation Agency awarded Taquan Air Service, Inc., a permit to operate an air taxi service between Annette Island and Ketchikan International Airport in southeast Alaska. Owner Jerry Scudero's market research indicated that he could get plenty of business transporting loggers, tourists, and state Fish and Game Department employees. Still, he balked at the $80,000 price of a seven-seat deHavilland Beaver airplane. Instead, he settled for a $40,000, four-seat Cessna 180.

The smaller aircraft limited the amount of work Taquan Air could accept. In addition, the wear and tear on the Cessna 180, trying to do too much with too little, cost the company a great deal of money for maintenance and repair. "I would have done a lot better more quickly if I had bought the larger plane," said Jerry, who was the company's only pilot in the early years. "I had so much freight in addition to people that I really loaded that 180 down. If I had bought a plane with more seats, I would have had more to sell." Taquan Air couldn't keep up with the business so, in 1980, the company bought a Cessna 185 and a year later added a deHavilland Beaver. "If you think the business is out there, make the financial commitment to the right equipment in the beginning because eventually you'll need it," Jerry advised.

During the mid-1980s, deregulation of the air charter industry brought enormous competition to Taquan Air's territory. While competitors slashed their prices, Taquan refused. It survived by strictly controlling costs and service area and maintaining high-quality service. Still, Jerry had learned his lesson about buying the needed equipment and facilities. He added four more aircraft by 1989. His strategy paid off. The company doubled its sales in 1986 and 1987 and upped them by 25 percent in 1988. By 1989, Taquan Air was the second largest air taxi service in Alaska, with seven aircraft, 45 employees, and $2.1 million in sales. Jerry also added land and maintenance facilities along the Ketchikan waterfront for his floatplanes. When the major competition closed its fixed-wing division in 1991, Taquan Air was prepared. The U.S. Forest Service awarded Taquan Air the contract to supply its fixed-wing air service in the Ketchikan region. The company doubled in size by the end of 1992. Investing in the right equipment and facilities made that growth possible, Jerry said.

In 1997 Jerry took his flight service in southeast Alaska in a new direction. He sold some of his shares in Taquan Air to buy most of the assets of Ketchikan Air, including hangers and leases at Ketchikan International Airport. Again, the purchase of the right equipment and facilities made it possible for Jerry to start a commuter airline to serve southeast Alaska. The air taxi service and commuter airline had a total of 40 airplanes. "It doesn't matter what business you're in, you have to get the right equipment to do the job," Jerry said. "You think 'I'm just a start-up. I have financial restraints.' But I know if I would have pressed it, I could have done something to obtain the bigger airplane [in the beginning]. While we were able to get past the initial years, we could have progressed faster."

28. SEIZE GROWTH OPPORTUNITIES

Some opportunities are best taken in the early years.

■ ■ ■

John T. Kott had a job refinishing appliances when he hit on an idea. Why not apply the same concept to sinks, bathtubs, and countertops? It would be less expensive and easier than replacing these items. However, no one was refinishing porcelain and fiberglass in 1953, so John had to develop the technology himself. That's when he started Kott Koatings, Inc. He and his son, John M. Kott, began franchising the concept in 1973 and selling international franchises in 1990. "We should have expanded into franchising 20 years earlier to spread our system across the country and overseas," said John M. "The cost obviously would be less and the expansion much greater because there was less competition and fewer governmental restrictions and paperwork in the good old days."

Some fledgling entrepreneurs buy franchises to gain instant experience, brand names, and proven systems of management. Some existing entrepreneurs sell franchises of their business packages as a way to grow their companies. Kott Koatings, headquartered in Foothill Ranch, California, was a service franchise (instead of a product franchise like McDonald's), which was a concept virtually unknown in the 1950s when the company began. Even when the Kotts started contemplating the idea in the early 1970s, only a few service franchises, such as H&R Block tax preparation and Roto Rooter plumbing, existed. "We went to a franchise attorney and said, 'Can this be done?' and he said, 'Sure, we can do anything,'" John M. said. "But it wasn't that easy." The basic business of refinishing porcelain remained the same, but the Kotts had to revamp and modify their procedures to guide franchisees. To maintain quality, the company sold its bathtub glazes only through its franchisees. "We had to train people to use our products because they depended on application technology," John M. said.

If Kott Koatings had figured out the franchising details in those early years, the company would have avoided fees and reporting regulations that most states now require. California, where Kott Koatings was located, adopted the nation's first law governing franchise investments in 1970. The Uniform Franchise Offering Circular was developed originally by the Midwest Securities Commissioners Association in 1975 and was monitored by the North American Securities Administrators Association. In 1989, the Federal Trade Commission chimed in with the first nationwide franchise disclosure regulation. Individual states adapted the uniform circular, so national franchisers had dozens of modifications with which to comply. These laws and regulations cropped up in response to investor complaints of abuses and deceptions by franchise sellers. It's not that the laws were unworthy, but they did complicate and add expense to the franchising process. Franchisers started avoiding some states, like Michigan, because their franchising rules and fees were so burdensome, John M. said.

Kott Koatings received so many purchase requests from foreign entrepreneurs that it started exporting its service franchises. This move brought on an entirely new regulatory process. The company's first effort was in

Canada because the country is so similar to the United States, John M. said. "We went through as many rules and as much paperwork, but after you go through it once, it becomes routine." The process was more complicated and costly in other countries. The U.S. Department of Commerce and consulates in various countries facilitated meetings in the countries, but negotiations took a long time, John T. said. Many foreign entrepreneurs had been burned by frauds with glossy brochures and nothing else to sell, so these potential buyers wanted to visit Kott's manufacturing plant to make sure the company was real. The Kotts endured this process and expense to achieve diversity. "We went into a wide range of countries so if the economy is bad in one country or region, we still have strong sales in other regions," explains John M.

Kott sold franchisees in more than 35 foreign countries and won national awards for outstanding export performance. Nevertheless, the Kotts believed their reach would be more expansive with less investment if they had seized the franchising opportunity two decades earlier.

29. AFTER THIS, WHAT?

Establish a retirement program in the early years of
business instead of waiting for a more affluent period.

■ ■ ■

Working in corporate America was a thankless grind for Gerard Moulin. For a decade after earning his engineering degree, Gerard worked for other engineering firms. His habit of working long hours eventually put him on a diet of heartburn medicine two or three times a day. "I was always salaried, so I didn't make any more by working more hours," Gerard said. "I decided if I was going to work so hard, it might as well be for myself."

So in 1986, Gerard established Ohm Corporation in Orange, California, an electrical and mechanical engineering firm specializing in heavy industrial and commercial projects. The company also prepares engineering studies for insurance companies and attorneys. Immediately, Gerard saved $60 a month, just on heartburn medicine.

Gerard's two regrets in his successful run were that he didn't start sooner. That is, he regretted the delay in starting his own company and then in saving for his retirement. Retirement just isn't uppermost in an entrepreneur's mind at the beginning of a venture, Gerard acknowledged. "But it should be," he said. "A friend tried to talk me into saving for retirement when I was in my 20s, but I said I didn't have any money."

Setting aside even a small amount each month can make a huge difference in the long run. For example, if you start setting aside $100 a month when you're 35, by age 65 you will have $95,103 (based on a modest 8 percent annual return on investment). Wait until you're 45 to start, and you'll have $34,604 at retirement. Start at age 55, and you'll have a paltry $7,348—hardly enough to retire on.

Gerard finally started putting money into an individual retirement account in 1990. However, IRA tax-deductible annual contributions were severely limited, so Gerard established a self-employed pension that allowed him to contribute as much as 15 percent of his income, also tax deductible. All employees had to be included in the plan as well. "I don't think you should shy away from giving employees a retirement plan," Gerard said. "It's cheaper than not giving yourself one." Gerard could have chosen a 401(k) plan, but the regulations and reporting requirements are complex for small companies. He also could have chosen a Savings Incentive Match Plan for Employees (SIMPLE). After Gerard established his SEP-IRA, the federal government approved a Roth IRA. Although the contributions to this plan aren't tax deductible, interest and future payouts are. Roth IRAs tend to be more suitable for people who have long investment times until retirement.

Investment advisors sometimes recommend using a combination of these plans, depending on each entrepreneur's financial and life circumstances. Gerard was unhappy he waited so long to begin saving for retirement. "My plan was to retire at 50. It didn't happen." However, he was satisfied with the plan he set up, and he applied the lesson he learned to the rest of his family. He set up retirement savings plans for all three of his children and his toddler granddaughter. "You need to have a long-term plan when you're young," Gerard said. "I know it's hard for a 20-year-old to think that way, but it's amazing how fast the years go by. Start a small plan and grow into it. You are your retirement."

PART 3

THE MONEY CHASE

■ ■ ■

Money is the new business's most obvious need. Yet even in this arena, new owners have many lessons to learn. The most important is how hungry a young business is for resources and how your money never goes as far as you imagined when it was just a gleam in your eye.

To begin, you must develop a system that enables you to understand exactly where your company stands financially. Fortunately, many low-priced, easy-to-use accounting software programs can explain the money side of your business. They can help you control your costs and live within your means, even if you own a business with wild seasonal gyrations.

If you don't have enough personal resources, you have to turn to those who do. They won't be as eager to part with their money as you think they should. You may pay dearly for use of their money. You may even find that you have to give them control over your business in exchange for their money.

Although the loudest entrepreneurial complaint regards the scarcity of money sources, perhaps the most problematic issue is pricing. As with early decisions, described in Part Two, the new business owner often lacks the confidence and experience to set a price that customers will pay and will allow the owner to make a profit. Hint: Most set their prices too low.

30.

WHAT YOUR FINANCIALS TELL YOU

To understand all the financial aspects of your business, learn to read and interpret balance sheets and income statements.

■ ■ ■

Anyone who loves to shop by mail probably knows the Lillian Vernon Corporation catalogs. They bring thousands of household, gardening, kitchen, Christmas, and other gift items to the at-home buyer. More than 1,300 year-round employees and thousands of seasonal workers send out $247 million in merchandise annually. It's hard to imagine that the whole thing started with a monogrammed purse and belt sold through a sixth-of-a-page ad in *Seventeen* magazine in 1951. Lillian designed and made the purse and belt with the help of her father, Herman Menasche, who owned a leather goods manufacturing plant in New York. Lillian was a 21-year-old pregnant housewife in need of more family income. To help make ends meet, she invested $495 of the money she had received as wedding gifts to buy the ad offering the purse for $2.99 and the belt for $1.99. Three dollars and two dollars seemed too pricy to Lillian, but $2.95 and $1.95 weren't profitable. Lillian's total investment was $2,000. She hoped for a $1,000 profit. Within the first three months, she received $32,000 in orders, and Lillian Vernon was transformed from a housewife to an entrepreneur.

However, lack of financial know-how hindered Lillian's decision making in building her mail-order company. She didn't even own an adding machine in those days, but a friendly banker let her use his once a week. "Understanding the financial aspects is the one area where I had little knowledge and experience in the 1950s," Lillian said. "Learning to read balance sheets and income statements before I launched my business would have helped."

These financial documents probably are foreign to someone who has never owned a business and, unfortunately, to some who have. A balance sheet details a company's assets (cash, inventory, equipment), liabilities (accounts payable, loans) and capital (equity in the business). The bottom line is the company's net worth. An income statement, often called a profit and loss statement, shows a company's financial performance over a period of time. This document breaks out every type of revenue and expense so the business owner can see trends. For example, if telephone charges are running higher than budgeted, the owner can investigate why and either take steps to control spending or adjust the budget to reflect the needed additional spending.

Even an entry-level college accounting class would have expanded Lillian's understanding of her accountant's calculations. Financial information helps the business owner develop a realistic budget, but its value is even more important in developing the vision for growth. "[My accountant] could tell me what was selling, but I needed to translate that information into decisions regarding production, advertising, and future expansion of product lines," Lillian said. She learned the financial side by trial and error and by hiring quality guidance through the formative years. Many of the early decisions Lillian made in her gut. With a gift for shopping, she added gold-plated pins and rings, a monogrammed bookmark that has remained one of the company's top sellers for more than four decades, and a brass doorknocker for homes with just one bathroom. In the 1960s, Lillian started enclosing a four-page, black-and-white catalog in orders, eventually expanding these catalogs until they were the major advertising and source of orders. The company later published eight full-color catalogs for different product niches, including "Christmas Memories" and "Lillian Vernon's Kitchen."

Lillian Vernon Corporation in New Rochelle, New York, which was sold to ZelnickMedia in 2003, sold products to more than 20 million customers worldwide including some well-know buyers. Singer Frank Sinatra ordered a monogrammed lint remover. Former First Lady Barbara Bush and actor/California Governor Arnold Schwarzenegger were also customers.

"Generally," Lillian said, "those entrepreneurs who see beyond their creativity and learn how to read the barometers of growing a profitable business have an excellent chance of success."

31. BE REALISTIC

Experts advise a start-up entrepreneur to develop conservative
financials, but being too conservative can work against you.

■ ■ ■

After 11 years as a police officer and one year as a security executive
for a large bank, Julie Russell decided in 2002 to open a detective agency,
Diversified Investigations LLC, in Appleton, Wisconsin. The company
provided a range of security and investigative services for corporate clients, drawing upon Julie's former police experience in financial crimes and
internal corporate thefts. She wrote a business plan for Diversified Investigations and worked diligently to predict income and expenses realis-
tically. This step is one of the most difficult for new business owners because they lack the experience to accurately predict their financials. Many
new ventures are built more on faith and enthusiasm than on actuality. Still,
Julie did her best. "I thought my revenue would be $500 a month for the
first six months," she said. "I actually did much better than I expected. I'm
double where I thought I'd be."

However, Julie discovered that her overly conservative numbers worked
against her. "I thought I would borrow the money to start the business," Julie
said. "When I showed my business plan to the bank, the banker said, 'You're
not going to make any money this year. We take your numbers and cut them,
because business owners always inflate their numbers.' I was shocked how
he looked at it."

Unfortunately, the banker was right. The typical business owner max-
imizes anticipated revenues, minimizes expected expenses, and makes no
allowance at all for unexpected costs or problems. This is most unfortunate
for the business owner. Your spending decisions will be more expansive if
you expect to be rolling in cash than if you expect to be eating beans for
dinner at the end of the month. The best approach is to use well-justified
assumptions when developing the basic financial projections—income
statements, balance sheets, and cash flow statements. Bank officers and
professional investors want to see the thought process behind the numbers
used to develop long-term projections.

One approach is to build your financials, as Julie did, from the bottom up. For example, you calculate that you will make two sales calls a day, resulting in at least two signed contracts per month for the first six months, increasing to four contracts per month by the end of the first year. Expenses will be bare bones, operating from a home office at first, with a used desk and computer, standard phone and answering machine, and entry-level e-mail address, and so forth. Then verify the reasonableness of your numbers two ways. First consider the size of your market and number of competitors, market share you can reasonably capture, and annual spending in your region for the products or services you provide. The second approach is to research financial comparisons on similar companies. Trade associations, research books, even colleagues in other markets can help provide numbers. The more precise your numbers, the more a banker or investor is likely to believe them. While you may use your research as the basis for a loan or equity investment, do the work for yourself as the basis for your day-to-day decision making and long-term strategic planning.

Julie launched Diversified Investigations without the banker's help. She lived frugally, worked hard, and followed her business plan. She quickly outstripped that plan, both financially, and in staffing needs. By the end of her first year, Julie had two employees. "I loved being self-employed," Julie said. "Being Christian, I thought this happened for a reason. This area was growing and needed an investigative service with my experience. It gave me an opportunity to help people."

32. EVERYTHING COSTS MORE THAN YOU THINK

How much money do you think you need
to start your business? Double it.

■ ■ ■

Lawrence Rouse quit his job in Illinois in 1978 and moved to Kansas. His plan was to run three companies for a client while he built up his own financial and management consulting firm. "Timing was bad," Larry said. "The economy went down the tubes, and my client sold his businesses. I hadn't had enough time to establish my own practice. I had $1,500 in my pocket. It was ugly."

Larry moved back to Chicago, where he knew relatives would at least feed him, and started doing subcontracting work for other consultants. That was the inauspicious beginning of Associated Enterprises, Ltd., later relocated to Lakewood, Colorado. The company took five years longer than Larry anticipated to get rolling because he tried to start on a shoestring budget, with little working capital to carry him through that unexpected financial loss. "I wasn't totally stupid, but bad timing caught up with me," Larry said. "Almost inevitably it takes longer than you think to get established, and just when you need to make a professional impression, you run out of advertising money, clean suits, and business cards." As fast as he could, Larry built a cash reserve earmarked for emergencies only. Then he kept at least three months of operating capital in the bank at all times on the principle that a company never knows when unexpected expenses will come up or the economy will go down.

Larry knew his start-up experience wasn't unique because he did so much work finding financing for young companies. He also did business valuations, expert witness services for legal action, and general consulting. One of his client companies had $20 million in sales but was strapped for cash. "Every time [company management] opened a subsidiary, it should have set up a reserve fund for unexpected expenses," he said.

Each industry is different, but Larry said a good rule of thumb is to build up enough money to pay your bills for at least two months. Many customers don't pay for 30 or 60 days, so even a bustling business has to survive until the cash flows in. "When I was still in Chicago, a major phone center went out for six months," Larry recalled. "For companies totally dependent on their phone systems, this was terrible. It was three or four months before they got any money back from the phone company. By then, some were out of business. "You never know what's going to occur."

When the economy booms and your business grows, start planning for the next downturn, Larry advised. In good times, stock up on letterhead stationery and office supplies. Lease rather than buy computers to conserve capital. "A lot of companies are not prepared," he said. "They wake up one morning, need money, and they've never met their bankers." If necessary, force your bank to allow you to meet with bank officers, and then send the officers quarterly financial statements. "So when you need a loan, you don't have to start from scratch," he said. "You have someone who understands your company." Also, start-ups should hire financial advisors used to working with small businesses. "The small-business accountant will do the same work as one used to working with established companies and will call to warn that your quarterly taxes will be due next week or ask why a particular expense was so high last month."

33. A CUSHION TO START

Having contracts in hand before starting your
business gives a tremendous boost to success.

■ ■ ■

Carl Bailey had owned a variety of small businesses when he noticed that many large companies and organizations were looking for specialty items with strong identification value. He decided, in 1993, that custom-made ties and scarves bearing a group's logo or name were ideal for this purpose.

However, a product supplier can go broke waiting for retailers to pay for merchandise. "At first, I had a lot of inventory out on the street," Carl said. "I'd walk into stores, and my ties would still be on the rack. I'd be having a heart attack." Instead, he should have started J.C. Neckwear & Scarves, located in Philadelphia, Pennsylvania, with enough orders in hand for 6 to 12 months' operating capital, Carl theorized. "That would have taken unnecessary pressure off, so I could devote time to seeking new contracts and completing current contracts."

Carl explained his lack of a capital cushion to his banker, who was willing to arrange a line of credit, and to his suppliers, who were willing to give him better credit terms and flexibility to bring in some revenue before he had to pay their bills. Carl also changed his focus so that he dealt strictly on custom orders. He didn't have any up-front inventory manufacturing or storage costs. "I sold the ties before I made anything," he said.

Too many fledgling entrepreneurs start their ventures before they find out whether anyone wants what they have to sell, said Carl, who also did volunteer business counseling with minorities. "What I tell people to do before they start is test the market," Carl said. "Go to people who will be your customers, and see if they will buy what you have."

The double benefit of up-front orders is receiving start-up operating capital and gaining market research that validates your business concept. Some people will make valuable comments that help you clarify your idea, modify your product or service, or hone your target market. However, asking would-be customers to pay for product before you have any is tricky. To compensate, you must have a carefully crafted concept and some samples. You also should research the most likely buyers.

Carl learned that private clubs, country clubs, and universities were receptive to his custom ties and wanted to buy them in quantity. This knowledge was important to his strategy of obtaining sales before manufacturing product. It wouldn't be cost effective to produce a handful of ties. Carl also discovered markets within markets: not only did the University of Pennsylvania want custom ties, the medical school and business school wanted their own unique designs. When an exclusive men's club in Washington, D.C., admitted its first women members, representatives from the organization sat down with Carl to design a club scarf to complement the custom ties J.C. Neckwear & Scarves already provided.

"My business was really made by being creative with customers' ideas," Carl said. "At first, I paid someone else to design the ties, but my manufacturer said the best touch was to do it myself. I knew what to look for in design." Always looking to expand his knowledge and efficiency, Carl took computer graphics courses to learn how to create his tie and scarf designs using modern technology. "I'm not that artistic," he said. "I'm proof that anyone can take a business, no matter what it is, and make it a success if they are willing to put in the time."

34.

LIVE WITHIN
YOUR MEANS

Every start-up business benefits from
following a realistic budget.

■ ■ ■

The recession of the early 1990s gave Maureen Murphy two options: relocate or start her own mail-order catalog consulting firm. Because owning a business had been her dream, Maureen chose the latter in 1995, establishing Murphy Marketing in Santa Monica, California (now Direct Effectz in Irvine, California).

Maureen had an idea how much her revenues would be and what expenses she would incur, but she did not create a realistic business budget at first. That was a costly mistake. Even a home-based consulting practice had greater expenses than Maureen imagined. She had wrongly assumed she would live on less. "I overspent at the beginning, partly because I didn't realize how fast my start-up capital would be depleted just with basic expenses," she said.

While Maureen didn't make the common start-up mistake of ignoring her financials, she did something just as dangerous. She didn't believe them. "For the first year, every time I reviewed my expenses, I would say to myself, 'But this isn't my real budget. I will spend much less once I've gotten this kicked off,'" she said. Maureen underestimated most expenses, especially taxes. She also aimed too low for her revenue goals. Although this seems to be a happy mistake, unrealistic revenue goals, based on underestimated expenses, can hold a company back. "There was no reason to set such modest income goals," she said.

Maureen finally put her business spending and income on a simple bookkeeping software program. "I figured out my actual costs instead of just what I thought [they were]," Maureen said. "I could see that I wasn't being extravagant, and that I wouldn't get by on less money eventually. I had to increase my revenues." That's when she started reviewing her business cash flow and other financial reports monthly and, for an overview, annually. From past experience, Maureen could forecast future expenses. "When I really knew how much I needed to earn to survive and to flourish, I took the steps to earn the money," she said. "When I began to target higher financial goals, I started achieving them."

Without an accurate budget, Maureen's initial approach to her business was skewed. She started consulting in all areas of direct mail advertising, because she thought her areas of expertise, mail order and cataloging, were too narrow to sustain her business. Over time, Maureen discovered that although her market had fewer catalog firms than companies using direct mail to generate sales leads, the catalogers needed her skills more on an ongoing basis. These long-term contracts were more lucrative than one-time projects. She also found she could command higher pay in a specialized area than in trying to serve everyone in direct mail.

Maureen, like many consultants, discovered that client demands for her knowledge exceeded the time she had to give. Therefore, she created a monthly forum through which she coached professionals in the mail-order industry. Also to maximize the use of her time, Maureen taught classes and seminars in mail order and cataloging. "A financial consultant looked at my results and called them wildly successful," she said, "but I thought I could still make quite a bit more by getting more ongoing projects and [giving more] classes."

35. CASH IS KING

A new business must create cash flow to survive.
Even profitable businesses fail if they run out of money.

■ ■ ■

Wisconsin is known for cheese and football and ginseng. You don't believe it? Paul Hsu didn't either in 1972. The native of Taiwan's Pescadore Island was well acquainted with the gnarly brown root that the Chinese have used for centuries to cure everything from anemia to insomnia. Then a friend showed Paul an article stating that 90 percent of American ginseng was raised in Marathon County, Wisconsin. "My mom was ill. Bearing 14 children had taken a lot out of her. So I sent her two pounds of American ginseng," said Paul, who was working as a social worker for the state of Wisconsin at that time. "My father wrote back—they didn't have a phone—six months later and said Mom's health was improved. She slept better, walked better." That convinced Paul to start Hsu's Ginseng Enterprises, Inc., a part-time ginseng distribution business, and to plant his first ginseng crop in 1973.

The good part of ginseng farming was the $45 to $65 a pound Asians would pay for the crop. The bad part was that the farmer must invest as much as $125,000 an acre and wait four years to harvest a crop. And land could be used only once to raise ginseng. Now that's a cash flow headache. "No cash flow can kill a business," Paul said.

Most fledgling business owners don't realize that even a profitable company can go bankrupt without cash flow. Profit is an accounting principle. You pay your bills and employees with cash, not profit. Furthermore, you must have the cash at the right time. If you must pay workers each week and your bills each month, but your customers don't pay you for 60 or 90 days—or four years, in Paul's case—the business has a cash flow lapse that you must plan for.

Cash forecasting is a record of known expenses in future months. That record helps the new business owner avoid overspending whenever a big check arrives, only to starve a month later when the annual insurance premium is due. Without such planning, the company misses profit opportunities, hurts its credit rating, and eventually goes bankrupt.

To give himself cash flow until his own crops matured, Paul started selling ginseng raised by other farmers. "I borrowed from my mother-in-law, friends, relatives. Five years later, I was finally able to get a loan," Paul said. "Finally I got a line of credit, so I no longer have cash flow problems."

Most Americans buy Chinese ginseng because it's cheaper than the American counterpart. Paul looked toward Hong Kong, Taiwan, Singapore, Malaysia, and China, where Wisconsin ginseng is prized because it's stronger. "North American ginseng had a light, bitter taste with a touch of sweetness; it had a more herbal flavor," he said. "I believe those differences made North American ginseng a saleable alternative across the Pacific. "Exporting also helped a domestic company weather periodic economic downturns," Paul said.

Paul's strict control of costs and cash flow helped grow Hsu's Ginseng Enterprises into the United States' largest ginseng exporter, with annual sales of $20 million, almost a third of the total U.S. ginseng exports. The company owned a thousand acres, although it cultivated only 160 acres at a time. "Most people don't realize the commitment in time and effort a small business requires," Paul said, "and the stomach for risk."

Thank goodness for the antistress characteristics of ginseng.

36. KEEP AN EYE ON THE MONEY

Continually monitor your spending and income and make
necessary adjustments immediately to remain profitable.

■   ■   ■

Dianne Santeford started making and buying gift items and reselling them to retailers in the 1980s. Hearts and Flowers, Inc., literally started at the kitchen table of her Maryville, Washington, home. The wholesale business did well until the Beanie Babies craze pulled most of the retailers' purchasing dollars away from other products. That fad left wholesalers like Hearts and Flowers, Inc., with too much inventory and too little cash. "In the gift industry we must make our buying decisions four to six months in advance to import from China," Dianne said. "Stores were leaving eight feet of shelves empty until their Beanie Babies arrived because they didn't have any money to buy other inventory."

Dianne decided she needed a simple, yet accurate means to track her inventory and capital to help her make accurate buying decisions. This continual monitoring of cash flow is important because companies can be highly profitable on paper but flat broke. The move saved Dianne's business. Many small-business owners count the money in the cash register at the end of the day and figure that is their profit. Those owners don't survive long in business. The survivors set up paper ledgers or buy accounting software, even something simple like QuickBooks, by Intuit. Dianne created her own system using Microsoft Excel. "The program I developed was simplistic in format, an annual way of tracking all income and expenditures," she explained. "Anticipated expenses and income for each week were plugged into the program for as much as 12 months in advance. As new expenses arose, I entered them into the spreadsheet and the totals automatically changed. I could see on a weekly basis how my cash flow stood. Spending too much? Don't have enough money left in the credit line to meet demand? I could make decisions based on fact, not desire."

Again, some business owners rarely monitor their cash flow. They have a bookkeeper enter the numbers, but don't do the vital analysis to spot trouble while they can still make adjustments to save their businesses. A series of unexpected events between 2001 and 2003 greatly affected Hearts and Flowers, Inc., from the 9/11 terrorists attacks in New York and Washington, D.C., to recession, a West Coast dock strike, and the Iraq War. Without her financial tracking tools, Dianne would not have been able to react quickly enough to keep her company stable. She cut staff because payroll was her greatest expense. Her spreadsheets showed her how many additional days she could extend terms to her retail customers. Those who qualified were given a longer time to pay their invoices, which made them willing to buy additional merchandise. Because Dianne's system was so simple, she was able to turn it over to her daughters, who worked with her in the business. One handled the finances and the other did all the purchasing. "They worked hand-in-hand making sure this program was kept current and effective," Dianne said.

37. TRACK INVENTORY FOR PROFITABILITY

Track your inventory closely.
Don't keep anything that's not covering its costs.

■ ■ ■

After owning a liquor store, Larry Thompson decided to try his hand at a more sober business: gourmet coffee. He bought a Coffee Beanery franchise in a Newark, Delaware, regional mall in 1990. With just 764 square feet of space in the store, every inch had to yield maximum profitability. At first, Larry served brewed drinks and sold packaged coffee and tea, coffee makers, bean grinders, mugs, and other accessories. However, the merchandise mix was wrong, and his inventory costs were too high— 52 percent of sales. Typically, if a business's costs are too high, it either prices its merchandise higher or reduces its profit margin. Larry probably could have gotten away with the first strategy if his were the only gourmet coffee shop in town. But supermarkets, discount stores, convenience markets, even gas stations sell gourmet coffee, Larry pointed out. He couldn't price himself out of the market.

Some business pioneers have covered mistakes in their cost of goods with higher prices. For example, the first video stores sold blank videotapes for $18. Eventually, however, sharp-penciled competitors entered the market with better cost controls and captured sales with lower prices, driving the high-priced stores out of business. The other option—lower profit margins—might work for a business with large volume, but a small shop won't produce a living wage if it lowers its profit margin too much. Nobody's in business to do that, at least not for long.

To get a handle on his costs and what merchandise was profitable and what wasn't, Larry set up his cash register to separate all his products into categories: coffee makers, grinders, and drinks served over the counter, which he broke down into subcategories such as café caramels and espresso-based drinks. This practice is common in retailing. Larry learned it from a grocery store where he worked while in college and later used it in his liquor store. At the end of each month, Larry got a printout that told exactly how much of each category had sold. He discovered that tea accounted for less than 2 percent of his sales. He didn't sell many coffee makers, and after the first months, bean grinder sales dwindled.

Retailers try to achieve a certain dollar volume in sales per square foot. They reduce or eliminate merchandise that doesn't meet their goals. Based on the Coffee Beanery's inventory tracking, Larry said, "We cut back on the tea we carried. We reduced the number of grinders we carried from three to one, and we didn't sell coffee makers at all anymore. That provided more space for packaged gift sets." He made room for 50 types of coffee beans. Beverages quickly grew to 60 percent of Larry's sales, compared with 40 percent in 1990. Cost of goods dropped from 52 percent to 39 percent. Larry's shop was the number one franchised location among more than 200 for Coffee Beanery.

For a single-location store whose owner works in the business, monthly is probably often enough to evaluate costs and inventory, Larry said. "Talk to the customers. They'll tell you what's selling." However, customer habits can vary widely with location. Other Coffee Beanery locations are in airports, on streets, and in shopping center kiosks that are even smaller than Larry's shop. "A street-front shop might sell more packaged foods, like sandwiches, than I did and might carry only 12 types of beans."

A business owner also can use sales and inventory information to market the business, Larry said. "My cash register could tell me how many eight-ounce cups I sold to mall employees. Should I run specials on that? Should I push 12-ounce cups? Should I give mall employees mugs so they'll be traveling ads for my business? "Having the information is great, but you must evaluate it, too," Larry advised.

38. PRICING A PRODUCT

Price your products to make a profit.
It's difficult to raise prices later.

■ ■ ■

Trish Kasey was a human resources manager, but when her daughter was born in 1991, Trish wanted to stay home with her. Inspired by Amy Dacyczyn, publisher of "The Tightwad Gazette" newsletter, Trish decided she could publish a newsletter for moms, whether they worked or stayed at home. "I had absolutely no idea what to charge for subscriptions," she said. "Instead of researching how much it would cost to produce [my newsletter, I researched] comparable newsletters. They charged $12 to $15 a year, so I figured I should charge $12." Trish overlooked the fact that those other newsletters were published quarterly, and hers was a monthly. The first edition of "Mommy Times," published in Trish's Newport Beach, California home hit the mailboxes in 1992. Trish had no idea whether she could make any profit at $12 per subscription. After the publication grew from four pages to ten pages, she couldn't. She also learned that she couldn't keep subscribers if she raised her prices—not because her newsletter wasn't worth it, but because people had already been persuaded that it was worth $12 a year.

Price is an elusive number, but you should figure it out before you start. Then show a sample of your product to some potential customers and ask whether they would be willing to pay your price. If not, and you can't cut your costs or are unwilling to cut your profits, you shouldn't start the business. It's as simple as that.

Here's a simple formula for calculating your price for a product: Multiply the cost of material and labor by the number of units you want to make each year. Add all other costs. Add your desired profit. Divide the result by the number of units. The answer is the price you must charge.

Those "other costs" can be deal killers. For "Mommy Times," they included printing, postage, advertising, delivery costs, office supplies, and sales and income taxes. If Trish wanted to research the price for "Mommy Times" before she started publication, based on 1,000 expected subscribers, her calculations would have been as follows: Materials and labor of $2 per newsletter cost $24,000 ($2 times 1,000 subscribers times 12 issues a year). Add indirect costs of $36,000. Add a desired profit of, say, $12,000. The total is $72,000. Divided by 1,000 units, this figure breaks down into an annual subscription cost of $72.

Trish realized she would go broke if she continued publishing "Mommy Times" the same old way. She had to cut costs. When a friend who had a Web site for his real estate company offered to host a "Mommy Times" site on the Internet free of charge to Trish, she jumped at the opportunity. The site went up in October 1995, and the response was huge. The site included an e-mail advice and comment section, articles of information, and support for mothers. "I was reaching thousands of mothers worldwide instead of hundreds across the United States," she said. The electronic "Mommy Times" made money by selling products for moms and babies through a virtual mall set up by an Internet commerce company in exchange for a percentage of sales. The Internet store required no inventory, so it added no up-front costs or interest and warehouse charges to the business.

39. PRICING A SERVICE

Time is more valuable than money.
Be sure to price your time accordingly.

■ ■ ■

Quick Tax & Accounting Service started in St. Louis, Missouri, because of a family fight. Roy Quick, at the time a corporate accountant, wanted to buy a new Macintosh computer. No way! The kids are entering college and we need the money, replied his wife, Edith, a junior high school teacher at the time. So Roy started preparing tax returns at night and on weekends to pay for his computer and software. "The first year [1984], we had one client who was my best friend," Roy said. However, the business soon grew to the point that Roy could quit his corporate job and join Edith full time. The toughest part, they both agreed, was realizing—and charging for—the full value of their expertise and services.

Undercharging and giving away too much service and advice are among the biggest causes of financial ruin for service businesses. "You want the business so badly, and then clients try to intimidate you into lowering your price," Roy said. But, Edith added, "It's a big mistake for services to try to be the cheapest."

In theory, to calculate its prices, a service provider starts with the annual income it wants to make and adds total costs. It then figures out billable hours each year (generally 20 percent to 50 percent less than the hours actually worked). The company divides income plus costs by billable hours. The result is the hourly rate the service provider must charge. In practice, that hourly rate may have to be modified by competitive pressures. If you don't want to ask competitors what they charge, ask their clients what they pay. Many trade associations keep track of standard industry pricing as well.

The Quicks finally set a minimum price on tax returns they prepared. If a client balked, the Quicks referred that client to another tax preparer. Roy and Edith also looked at the "hassle factor." Clients who were disorganized, required hours of research to complete their tax work, called dozens of time for free advice, and were unpleasant to work with were a hassle and, therefore, more costly to have as clients than organized and friendly clients. "You must identify your unprofitable clients promptly and change your billing method," Edith said.

After several years in business, Roy and Edith sat down after tax season and graded their clients—*A, B,* or *C.* The *A* clients were lucrative and pleasant. The *C* clients were hassles, to be replaced by *A*s, if possible. Some of the bigger clients were the easier ones to work with, the Quicks agreed, because they understood the value of ability, experience, and quality, all service intangibles. These clients didn't mind paying $200 for returns that saved them $1,000 in taxes and didn't trigger IRS audits. At the other end of the scale were clients like the man who was paying 12 percent interest on his home mortgage. When interest rates plunged and Roy suggested he refinance, the man saved $6,000 in interest over the year. However, the client was angry because the lower interest payment reduced his tax refund by $2,000 the next year.

The Quicks increased their fees over the years, which drove away a few of the troublemakers. They also added an up-front deposit that the customer must pay at the first appointment. "Service businesses sell knowledge," Roy said. "Once you've given that away, you have no leverage [to get paid]." Besides, Edith added, "If they won't pay you now, what makes you think they will pay you later?"

The Quicks also started accepting credit cards. "We were amazed how much we liked the results," Edith said. "We don't get bad checks, and the client can't say, 'Oh, I forgot my checkbook.'"

40. THE MONEY SEARCH IS ENDLESS

Trying to get a bank loan is one of the
hardest ways to finance a business start-up.

■ ■ ■

After earning a business degree and working two years at a health club, 23-year-old Tim Mansour decided, in 1985, to open his own health and fitness club in his hometown of Rome, Georgia. He had limited capital, so Tim approached a local bank for a loan. Then a second. Then a third. In all, more than 50 banks turned down Tim's loan application. "I was asking for a million dollars, and I didn't have a great business plan," Tim admitted. Also, bankers were skeptical because Tim was so young, and no one wanted to finance a health club, a business in which 20 start-ups fail for every one that succeeds.

Often, persistence alone does not bring success in landing the financing a new business owner requires. Even today, banks are not great friends of business start-ups, but in the mid-1980s, most weren't even on speaking terms with small businesses in general. Then, as now, bankers want business borrowers to prove their ability to repay loans. That usually requires a combination of experience, collateral, creditworthiness, profitable financial statements, and positive demographics. Start-up business owners have a tough time proving the worth of their ideas because they don't have at least three years of financial statements to demonstrate that they have been profitable, growing, and generating enough cash flow to meet monthly loan payments.

Tim's attitude was that no isn't an answer; it's just another obstacle. It was significant that Tim tried to learn from each failure. Every time a banker turned down Tim's loan application, he asked why. Then he improved his presentation for the next banker. "It's not what *you* want to tell the bank; it's what the bank wants to hear," Tim said. "Each wanted to know what I was planning to do in the next three to five years. So I added that. Then they wanted to know what I would do if I got into trouble." Finally, one banker suggested Tim contact the U.S. Small Business Administration (SBA). Since 1953, the SBA has guaranteed small-business loans made through banks and other commercial lenders. The government takes on some of the perceived additional risk of lending to smaller companies. But the SBA, too, wants evidence that loans will be repaid. "I don't think I ever would have gotten a loan without the U.S. Small Business Administration," Tim said.

With the help of a professional loan packager, Tim sharpened his concept so that he wasn't proposing just another gym, but a multipurpose fitness complex with swimming pools, racquetball courts, outdoor sundecks, childcare, weight rooms, cardiovascular machines, aerobic studios, lockers, steam room, sauna, and whirlpool. Tim would own the building. The business would compete on service and facilities, not on price. One of the smartest things Tim did while searching for a bank loan was to research his industry and the entire Southeast. A hometown friend suggested he try Gwinnett County, an Atlanta suburb, which was one of the fastest growing areas of the United States during the 1980s.

Research, a good business plan, and persistence finally paid off. Tim got an SBA loan to open the first Fitness International with three employees in Snellville, Georgia, in 1986. It was a 25,000-square-foot freestanding facility that grossed $650,000 in its first year. That club and a second one Tim opened in 1988 enabled him to pay off his SBA loan in five years. He took out another SBA loan for his third center in 1991 and built a fourth in 1994. The last three centers were almost double the original's size. "Having an excellent track record with the original health complex made funding the additional three complexes not as difficult," Tim said. "But it was still tough, even with years of successful experience."

41. EQUITY, NOT DEBT

Debt financing can stifle growth for a start-up firm because
repayment of debt is a considerable drain on earnings.

■ ■ ■

After 25 years' experience in financial institutions, Frank Shemanski
gave up his senior executive position to launch Southwest Financial Services, Inc., in Brea, California. The company leases merchant credit card
equipment and processes credit card purchases. It charges a 1 percent to 2
percent fee for each transaction in which a client accepts a credit card for
payment. Frank knew the industry and the job before he started his company. He had worked for banks of all sizes and created a financial services
division for one employer, not unlike starting a company. However, when
he began Southwest Financial in 1988, he didn't have the deep pockets of
a major corporation, so Frank borrowed $20,000 from family, friends, and
long-time business associates. Like many entrepreneurs, he didn't want to
give up any ownership or control.

But debt financing was a big mistake that drained limited resources,
Frank said. For example, he was paying 8 percent to 15 percent interest on
the loans. "Using debt instead of equity resulted in paying interest on
money that we had not yet put to work generating income, thus creating an
expense that affected profits and diluted net worth of the company," Frank
said. In addition, the initial capital gave an illusion of wealth that the start-
up company did not yet have. Southwest Financial paid salaries equivalent
to corporate jobs and bought business equipment and furnishings that did
not generate income.

"We quickly recognized that we were expending capital at a faster
pace than the revenues were being generated, so we immediately tightened
our financial belts, obtained additional funding to replace the excesses, and
monitored our results on a daily basis," Frank said. He went to his initial
debt holders and asked them to convert their loans to equity in the company. All agreed because Frank could demonstrate that for a little more
risk, they would likely get higher returns on investment as the company
continued to grow. The change boosted Southwest Financial in two ways:
The company no longer had to use income to pay interest and principal,

and the extra equity improved the company's net worth on its financial statements. "Tight management, effective planning, and a lot of long hours and hard work got us over the hump," Frank said.

The experience made Frank an advocate of running a company with the help of both a business plan and a budget based on the amount of investment capital available. These documents help the owner resist the temptation to spend money on products and activities that do not contribute to making money. New business owners, especially those who have been used to the perks of high executive positions, are tempted to lease fancy offices, equip them with lavish furniture, and pay themselves high salaries. A budget helps an owner differentiate between what the company must have to survive and the luxuries that will have to wait.

After righting the ship, Southwest Financial started enjoying double-digit growth each year, processing more than $100 million in purchases a month. The company was profitable every year. While retailers have been the backbone of the $500 billion credit card industry, the company benefited from large numbers of manufacturers, distributors, and even government agencies that now accept credit card payments. Secured purchases on the Internet were another growth segment.

42. GIVE A PIECE OF THE ACTION

Even if you're willing to give up part of your venture
to gain working capital, you may not find any takers.
Figure out an alternative.

■ ■ ■

Jim Dartez was an engineer by training and a medical instrumentation salesperson by experience when a large conglomerate approached him about saving one of its divisions that made water quality monitors. What he found was a money-losing manufacturer with stagnant growth and disgruntled employees. The entire industry suffered from unreliable technology for monitoring the quality of water that waste treatment plants and water companies didn't trust. Jim proposed a three-year turnaround plan that involved moving the division to New Orleans, Louisiana, and starting from scratch with new employees and new technology. Just as he started implementing the plan, another company began buying up the conglomerate's stock. So, in 1987, Jim and his wife put every dime they had into buying the division to create Royce Technologies. "I should have given up some of the company to have cash to work with," Jim said. "We would have grown faster, though it might not have been better. Outside investors tend to micromanage. They don't know what you're doing, but they do know their money is at risk."

Keeping such investors informed and happy takes management resources, Jim said. Entrepreneurs must weigh the financial largess against this time commitment. On the other hand, a company gets a tremendous lift if the owner can attract the right investor with expertise in finance, marketing, or the venture's needed technology. Many private investors, who made their fortunes building companies before cashing out, look for companies that need their knowledge as well as their money.

But even with diligent searching and good professional relationships, most entrepreneurs can't find this type of investor. "I was so ignorant about finance, I probably would have danced to any drum around. But no one was beating the drum. No one had confidence in what I was doing. It's good that I didn't run into someone from the Mafia at the time," he joked. Instead, Jim and his wife risked everything. When Royce Technologies ran into financial trouble because it did a poor job collecting receivables, Jim's wife stepped in to correct the problem. However, Royce Technologies' basic problem ran even deeper than unpaid receivables. In the mid-1980s, water quality monitoring instruments were so poorly designed that customers hated them. Therefore, Jim hired aerospace and telecommunications engineers who knew nothing about water and everything about developing monitoring instruments. They applied techniques from other industries to create new water analyzers. That work took two years and in the meantime, Royce Technologies had to survive on its revenues because Jim didn't have any cash reserve. "We were selling ratty old stuff that wasn't very great—although it was as good as anything else on the market—but we really supported our customers and replaced things that didn't work," Jim said. "When our new instruments came out, our customers were willing to try them because we had done a good job for these people."

By 1991, Royce Technologies' portable analytical instruments became the U.S. benchmark for reliability and accuracy in water quality monitoring. Even before that time, however, Jim was aware that global markets, in addition to U.S. markets, would be important stabilizers for his company in the 1990s and beyond. "When you have an economic lapse in one part of the world, other areas are strong or in flux," he said.

43. WHAT'S WRONG WITH A MILLION-DOLLAR CONTRACT?

Outside investors can bring more than money into
the early stages of a new-technology venture.

■ ■ ■

A long-term goal of starting their own company sent Joyce and David Freiwald on a long-term mission to develop the management skills they would need for successful entrepreneurship. Their research told them that lasers would be one of the fast-growth segments of technology, so Joyce took a job in business development for a research and development company in the oil industry. David ran a laser division for a large defense contractor. When that company decided to bail out of the laser project, the Freiwalds decided it was time to start their own company in 1992. F2 Associates used lasers to remove coatings, such as paint or glue, from large surfaces. The process was environmentally safe. "We sold our house in San Diego, California, moved to New Mexico, and used our severance pay to start this company," said Joyce, who became president of the new venture. David became vice president in charge of technology development.

F2 Associates quickly earned multimillion-dollar contracts from the Department of Energy and the Air Force. The agencies wanted a demonstration of the effectiveness of the company's technology. Those contracts would appear to launch the new company toward certain success. Instead, they propelled F2 Associates into the awkward adolescent stage. In building their management and technology experience, Joyce said, they overlooked the need to understand how the financial game was played. "I wish that I had known earlier about the process, problems, and players in raising capital," Joyce said. "I could have avoided a lot of expensive mistakes."

The usual bank loans were not appropriate for high-tech firms like F2, she said. The amount of money the company needed to commercialize its technology was too large to raise from friends, family, and individual investors. Economic development programs in small states like New Mexico were inadequate for the technology firm's needs. Also, venture capital groups worked in narrow niches, so finding the right fit was time consuming and difficult. "Some investor groups want to be in before the technology is developed. We developed the technology before trying to get outside investors," Joyce said. "At that point they want to see commercial sales before they invest. One investor group would say, 'You're too mature for us.' And another would say, 'You're not mature enough.' And investors have niches within technology. They want biotech or software; we're neither."

Venture capitalists, many of whom manage funds for individuals, pension funds, and insurance companies, look for industries in which they are experienced and knowledgeable. Not all specialize in high-tech sectors; some like retailing or consumer products. Regardless of the industry, these professional investors look for high growth, typically 30 percent to 50 percent a year, in companies from which they can pull out their money by selling stock to the public within five to seven years. The typical venture capitalist reads a hundred business plans for each one invested in. Venture capitalists and wealthy private investors rarely put their money in companies that don't come highly recommended by experts they trust, like attorneys and accountants. Many of these experts make lucrative livings by playing matchmakers for cash-hungry young companies.

"You have to kiss a lot of frogs," Joyce said. "I learned to avoid the middlemen who want to be paid up front or to be paid a monthly fee in return for their help in seeking capital. I worked only with those who were willing to work on a contingency basis."

In 1998, the Freiwalds gave up majority ownership of F2 Associates to an investment group, which used a shell corporation to take the company public. This status gave investors a market in which to sell their shares if they wanted out and gave the company greater credibility with financial managers. The financing also helped the company pursue strategic relationships with major companies that have the markets established for the laser cleaning process. "It wasn't my first choice," Joyce said, "but we needed to do something to raise the millions of dollars needed to commercialize the technology."

44. DIGGING OUT OF EARLY HOLES

An undercapitalized start-up has to beg and
borrow to keep the company afloat.

■ ■ ■

In the mid-1980s, Gail Johnson was a college nursing instructor
yearning to do something more meaningful with her life. Then Gail met a
couple who had built their lives around their new baby daughter. When the
infant was diagnosed with susceptibility for sudden infant death syndrome,
they could not find childcare willing to take responsibility for the little girl.
"The mom was so upset, and I thought there was no reason to feel this kind
of pain," Gail said. She decided to combine her nursing skills and love of
children to establish a childcare program that would serve children both
with and without special health needs. Gail's attitude was positive: Her father had owned a fuel oil company when Gail was a teenager. Her husband
owned an engineering firm. If she wanted to start her own business, well,
of course she could.

Gail's husband did the design work for her new venture, and his company absorbed many of the prestart-up costs Gail otherwise would have
had to pay. One of his business associates, a real estate developer, agreed
to finance construction of the building, which Gail would repay through
rent. Rainbow Station opened in Richmond, Virginia, in 1989 with 18 children. It needed 95 to break even. Then the economy took a nosedive. "My
husband could no longer afford to absorb my costs," Gail said. "I remember thinking, 'Oh, my gosh! What have I done?'" Gail used her two Mas-
terCards and some savings bonds to try to save the company. As each new
child enrolled, the money went to pay the bills. But after six months, Rainbow Station was broke. Gail tried to renegotiate her lease, pointing out that
her rent was far more than the market rate. The landlord said that was the
price she had to pay for his up-front financing. "Finally, he said he'd evict
me, and I said, 'Do what you have to, but I can't pay,'" Gail said. "I knew
he couldn't use the building for anything else because it had been built to
our specifications." In the end, they worked out a deal to add the unpaid
rent to the end of Gail's lease term. In addition, Rainbow Station had to pay

exorbitant liability insurance rates because of the special nature of the clientele. The first-year premium was as much as the company would later pay for three childcare centers, once it had established a safe track record.

Rainbow Station survived financial starvation "only by the grace of God and a never-say-die attitude," Gail said. Fortunately, the childcare provider met a huge need in the Richmond area, and Gail had done a good job marketing its services to working parents. By the end of the first year, the center had 117 students, enough to pay the bills. Demand was strong for Rainbow Station's blend of accredited early childhood education and registered nursing staff. At the grand opening for the first center, the owner of an office park offered to give Gail land for a dollar if she would build a second center in the park. Gail went to the phone book and started calling banks. When she got to the *N*s, a young loan officer at NationsBank agreed to visit Rainbow Station. "She became our advocate and, I found out later, the sole reason I got the loan," Gail said. The second Rainbow Station was 90 percent filled within nine months. The third and fourth were in the black immediately. "None of this has been easy," Gail said. "You have to be willing to move forward in spite of obstacles. Never give up."

PART 4

MANAGEMENT ISSUES

■ ■ ■

You really know that you're a business owner when you make management decisions without looking around for someone else to tell you what to do. It's harder for some to make these decisions than others.

Your business will become the accumulation of management decisions you make. The suppliers will be the ones you find. The distributors will be the ones you woo. The business will accomplish its work under the guidelines you set up.

When you make your management decisions, adopt the as-if principle. If you act as if you are the owner of the most polished, professional, significant company in your industry, it will tend to be the truth. If you act as if nobody would buy from you—the person who flunked third grade math and never so much as served as hall monitor—that will tend to be the truth, too.

However, the fact you must never forget is that just because you're the owner doesn't mean you should be the sole decision maker. Your customers are the ultimate judges of your management decisions. So base your decisions on how you want your customers to see your products and services. Your decisions should always strive to satisfy and serve the customers.

45. INVESTIGATE BEFORE CREATING RELATIONSHIPS

Select alliances with individuals or groups whose beliefs, ethics, and desires match yours.

■ ■ ■

Doug Porter had worked in the printing industry for two decades, but his long-time dream was to be his own boss. In pursuit of that dream, the Placentia, California, resident attended a presentation for a network marketing company as a possible avenue to self-employment. The concept is that a company sells its products through independent distributors who are paid a commission not only on the products they sell themselves but the products sold by people they recruit into their "network" of distributors. This approach has used several different names: direct marketing, multilevel marketing, and network marketing, among others.

Doug didn't sign up immediately. "The company was not very ethical. They were all about recruit, recruit, recruit and money, money, money. I learned that doing some homework on the company would benefit me a great deal," he said. He was right. The Federal Trade Commission periodically issues warnings for potential entrepreneurs to be cautious, first about products that claim miracle cures and guaranteed results, and second about the parent company's marketing plan. Some are legitimate. Even companies like Gillette, AT&T, and Avon use direct selling. But others are pyramid schemes in which the first investors make a lot of money and later investors are left with nothing. The FTC warns against signing up with any plan that pays commissions for recruiting additional distributors into what is called your "downline"; that requires purchase of expensive products and marketing materials; that guarantees profits based on your downline; whose sales meetings apply enormous pressure to make an immediate decision; and that require minimum monthly sales.

"There were many ethical network marketing businesses to choose from," Doug said after doing extensive homework. "It was a choice of which company fit my beliefs, passions, and desires best." He chose Nikken, a Japanese seller of health technologies and products founded in 1975, which had $1.5 billion in annual sales from more than 30 countries and 30 million customers. Nikken paid commissions for product sales, not recruiting new distributors. Distributors didn't have minimum sales requirements. More important to Doug was the company's emphasis on helping people, not just making a buck. "We were focused on educating people about preventative health care. I wouldn't have given this opportunity a second thought if it had not been for trying the products and seeing them help so many people I knew personally," he said. "My son was helped with his breathing problems, my wife with the fatigue of her multiple sclerosis, a family friend with fibromyalgia, and many other friends and family with everyday aches and pains. The relief of pain gave me a reason to share with other people I knew who were hurting. It became a mission to help others physically and financially."

Doug also liked the opportunity to work with other distributors, not against them. "In traditional business when you train an employee to know what you know, you create your own competition when they leave and open another business around the corner," Doug explained. "In network marketing, when you train others to know what you know, their success is your success. You want them to go duplicate your efforts. It's gratifying to know my success helps others. Not all companies have this same philosophy, and their desire only for money will cause their failure."

46. LEARN TO BE A RESOURCE

You can increase your value to customers by providing
resources beyond the products and services you sell.

■ ■ ■

When Judy Sherkow started Training Dynamics in Corona, California, in 1990, she wanted to be a general, do-it-all, business consultant. Her greatest fear was that if she turned clients over to another consulting firm, she would never see them again. "It took me a while to realize how important it was to be a resource to clients and not try to do it all myself and fail in the attempt," she said. In one eye-opening experience, Judy accepted an assignment to present a four-hour seminar. She spent a hundred hours preparing for the seminar because she wasn't experienced on the topic. When she calculated her hourly wage for the project, it was well below minimum wage. That's when Judy decided to define her specialties as training supervisory and leadership skills, employee motivation, and stress management.

New business owners often focus so much on selling their products and services that they lose sight of the long-term value of being a resource of information and referrals for other client needs. Judy quickly learned that she didn't have to meet every client request as long as she knew other sources that could. "When my clients called asking me for a service I didn't provide, I found someone who did and provided the client with a list of contacts to choose from," Judy explained. "That saved my clients time and effort trying to find qualified consultants and provided a measure of comfort to them since they trusted my judgment." When clients knew Judy would be a trustworthy resource, it served another benefit to her. "My long-time clients knew what I did, so they might call and say, 'We know you don't do sales training, but do you know who does?' If I had added that service, then I could tell them. It was a great opportunity I wouldn't have if they didn't treat me as a resource."

Judy stressed the importance of a business owner managing company resources to maximize strengths. "It didn't do me any good to do mediocre work. Sales training, for example, is very specialized. Why should I spend time to get up to speed on that when I knew trainers who were excellent at it?" she said. That resource management freed her to become even better at her own specialties.

Becoming a resource requires work and research. A business owner must study the industry, learn the suppliers of a wide variety of products and services customers might seek, and test these sources to gain confidence when making recommendations. If you point customers to a bad product or service, it will reflect poorly on you too. Judy became active in the Association of Professional Consultants so she could become familiar with the training specialties of other consultants as well as their strengths and weaknesses.

Judy stayed in touch with clients for whom she has done training in the past. When she first started Training Dynamics she asked about future projects she could do for the clients. "When I touched base with them, it was not just for me, but to find out what training or other things they needed that I could help them with," she said. "Sooner or later there would be something I could do for them. If I could still meet their needs by referring them to colleagues, work would eventually come back to me. Believe it. The important thing was that clients called *me* first."

47. ACT LIKE A PROFESSIONAL

Playing around at business can hold an
entrepreneur back from achieving greater success.

■ ■ ■

For Devon and Beverly Davis of Flower Mound, Texas, business began with a creative solution to a personal need. But they eventually discovered that a company is more than a product. Before starting a business, Devon drove a BMW M Roadster, a two-seat convertible. To cramp matters further, he insisted on carrying a full-size spare in the trunk, leaving no room for luggage. So he created a garment bag that hung from the back of the car's seat.

Beverly, who had her own consulting firm, P.O.V. Marketing, thought the hanging garment bag, which she dubbed The Auto Valet, was a great idea that they should market. The pair formed a limited liability company they named Cross Timbers Innovations. "However, we started the company as a hobby," Beverly said. "I knew the idea was good, but didn't realize early on its full potential. So we sort of 'played' at business for a time."

Many inventors and creative people are gung ho on the product creation side but don't fully commit on the business side. Perhaps it's inexperience or fear or inertia. But for a company to realize its full potential, the owners must commit themselves fully. It helped that the Davises took the formal, legal step of forming a limited liability company. It would have helped as well to give themselves titles, print up business cards, and invest enough capital to give Cross Timbers Innovations a real chance.

The Davises did hire an attorney for legal filings, but handled most of the work themselves. Devon developed a prototype, with the help of Beverly's mom. Beverly found a local sewing house to manufacture the product. Beverly designed the company logo and Web site. Devon, a software engineer, did the programming and e-commerce. He filed his own patent application. The pair shot their own photos for advertising collateral and the Web site. All this work was at night and on the weekends because they continued their day jobs.

"We financed the entire business launch ourselves. While it's nice that we were able to do this, it slowed us down and forced the business to take off more slowly," Beverly said. "It didn't hold us accountable to any financiers, which allowed us to move at the pace of 'hobbyists.' Since there was no financial discomfort, we weren't motivated to grow or succeed quickly. We didn't devote the resources early on to have professional help with planning, marketing, design, photography, and sales."

Rather than take a systematic approach to sales, the Davises tried to recruit friends to help sell the product. After several failed attempts, they knew they needed professional sales help. Soon they found a distributor who handled products for roadster owners. He liked The Auto Valet but thought his customers would want a high-end product. So Devon and Beverly developed a deluxe model with shoe bags. They had three products, inventory, an e-commerce Web site, and a distributor. But they were still playing around.

"After adding two more products, we finally woke up to the fact that we needed to start treating this as a business and not a hobby," Beverly said. She wrote a business plan, uncovering the market potential for small aircraft as well as cars. The plan also revealed the restrictions of the Internet, so they pursued more distributors in additional markets and launched a media blitz. If they had taken this professional, all-out approach from the beginning, Cross Timbers Innovations would have grown faster, Beverly said.

48. PREPARE FOR QUICK RESPONSE

Replying to customer requests in a timely way
requires creativity as well as fast action.

■ ■ ■

When Teresa Maerzke started Power-Fill in Kenosha, Wisconsin, in 1998, she thought she was in a service business. She remanufactured and refilled ink and toner cartridges for all major brands of copiers and printers. She stressed the environmental and cost savings over buying new cartridges. She offered free pickup and delivery within her core market area. She educated customers about the safety and dependability of remanufactured cartridges. Yet she soon discovered that busy customers wanted more than good, guaranteed service. They didn't have time to wait even a few days to get their refilled and remanufactured cartridges back. They needed instant turn around.

Americans have become used to fast service, instant answers, and immediate access. We have one-hour photo developing services, fast-food drive-through restaurants, and high-speed Internet access. In some cases, the rapid response isn't just a desire, but a necessity. So businesses of all sizes must meet that demand for instantaneous answers. In many cases, fast service or quick turnaround is the competitive advantage of smaller companies. Large bureaucracies sometimes can't react and retool swiftly, while nimble small firms can make instant decisions and take immediate action. But how to deliver fast service is not necessarily obvious. In Power-Fill's primary business, remanufacturing an ink or toner cartridge required cleaning or replacing numerous rollers and corona wires, and cleaning blades as well as removing any waste toner and refilling with new toner. That was hardly a while-you-wait process.

Teresa decided Power-Fill must keep a supply of remanufactured ink and toner cartridges on hand. "I was able to trade the customer its empty cartridge for one that was essentially new but at half the price," she said. However, she needed a supply of surplus and cartridges for this swift service response. That meant that Power-Fill had to step beyond its service roots to build inventory. Furthermore, the empty cartridges had to be inexpensive so that the company could still retain its promised 50 percent price savings over new cartridges.

Teresa's solution to build an inventory of empty cartridges required a resourceful technique. "I bought empty cartridges from schools, churches, or youth organizations for my inventory supply," she explained. "The organizations benefited from my purchases as a fundraising program that was pretty simple. They collected the cartridges and I paid for them. Everyone won. It wasn't a complete fix, but it was a very good start."

The program required Teresa to monitor the types of cartridges her customers used, track her inventory of recharged cartridges, and monitor the technological changes of printers. She didn't want to buy too many empty cartridges that she couldn't remanufacture and sell to customers.

She also didn't want to stockpile cartridges that were obsolete. She needed to control her inventory without sacrificing service that her customers had come to expect. Many cartridge rechargers are part-time businesses operated by novices who only replace the toner. "Recharging was our livelihood," Teresa said. "We had to do it right or we didn't pay the bills."

49. COUNT THE HOT DOGS TOO

Institute inventory control measures from the start.

■ ■ ■

If you look at CKE Restaurants, Inc., today, with its more than 3,200 Carl's Jr., Hardee's, La Salsa, and Green Burrito restaurants, it's hard to imagine the whole conglomerate started with a hot dog cart.

Carl Karcher had an eighth-grade education, a steady job as a bread truck driver, and burning ambition. On July 17, 1941, he borrowed $311 against his Plymouth and added $15 from his wife's household budget to buy a hot dog cart in Los Angeles, California, across the street from a Goodyear tire factory. Carl sold hot dogs, chilidogs, and tamales stored in an ice chest and heated on a steam table. His first-day sales totaled $14.75. A muffin tin served as the cash register.

Carl kept his bread delivery job, and even though his wife, Margaret, often worked the cart with their first baby asleep in the Plymouth parked next to the cart, they had two employees run the stand. Each man worked alone for an eight-hour shift, earning $12 a week. Carl arrived at 2:00 AM each night to collect the day's receipts and close up by stacking sheets of plywood around the cart. Soon Carl noticed that the night shift consistently made about 25 percent less than the $12 to $15 that he expected. When he stopped by the cart unexpectedly one evening to study the problem, he discovered the employee was using hot dog buns that Carl hadn't bought.

The employee, who confessed his scam, knew that Carl tracked inventory by counting the buns, which Carl purchased by the dozen, instead of the hot dogs, which he bought by the pound. The employee bought his own buns and used Carl's wieners and condiments to sell three dozen hot dogs "off the books" each shift, pocketing $3.60 per day. "I learned fast about food costs and inventory controls after that," Carl said. "To this day, I place integrity high among the traits of a good employee."

Employee theft is an even bigger problem for American businesses than it was in the pre–World War II economy. Accurate record keeping and inventory control are important tools for curbing employee theft; however, today's small-business owner must do more. Begin by comparing every check returned with the business bank statement to the general ledger. Examine the amount of each check, the signature on the check, and the endorser on the back. Unless you do all the record keeping, bill paying, and product ordering yourself, assign these duties to different people. Because many thefts and embezzlements are uncovered when the culprits aren't around to keep the scheme going, require employees to take regular vacations. Inventory management serves an important purpose beyond keeping employees honest, however. Good inventory control helps an owner avoid overbuying while keeping the best-selling merchandise in stock, and it eliminates slow-moving products.

Obviously, much more is at stake today with inventory at CKE, which is now public and Carl is no longer actively involved. A few years after starting the company, Carl switched from hot dogs to hamburgers and other food. The business grew by opening its own restaurants, by franchising, and by buying other chains.

50. MAKE A SUCCESS YARDSTICK

Set goals so you can measure the company's
progress and health at critical early stages.

■ ■ ■

Kenneth Jacobs was content to be an employee of a large security company until the owner prepared to sell it. "I saw the handwriting on the wall that the company would go through major changes," Ken said. "I was 37, and I thought if I ever wanted to try something on my own, this was the time."

In 1987, Ken started JMG Security Systems in Fountain Valley, California, to install burglar alarms and other security devices. Within two months, he had an ulcer. "I was so used to a healthy paycheck, and here I was with zero income and worrying about money and paying bills," Ken said. "Rather than worry day in and day out, I decided to set some performance goals for the next six months, then reassess where I was at that point." The only significance of six months was that he had enough money to live on for that length of time. "I didn't know if six months was long enough, but it gave me enough time to get my name out there and attract some clients," Ken said. "It was a mental game, but it totally relaxed me and freed me up to do my best work."

Some entrepreneurs fret about what goals to set. To start, they might use industry standards. Some trade groups keep track of performance averages. Dun & Bradstreet Corporation annually publishes *Industry Norms and Key Business Ratios,* which gives typical financial statements and key ratios, such as current assets divided by liabilities or annual net sales divided by inventory, for major industry segments. This book is available in many public libraries.

To Ken, however, the goal itself wasn't as important as the act of setting it. The important step was to have a benchmark against which to measure performance. "How do you know how you're doing if you don't have anything to measure your performance by?" he asked. Ken determined he wanted 10 percent of the security alarm business in his area within five years. "I had no idea what that meant," he said. Later he learned that even a 2 percent market share was huge. He didn't achieve his goal, but still became a significant player in the industry.

Initially, Ken wanted to make sure JMG Security Systems was increasing its revenues and adding accounts—the right kind of accounts. By his standard, this meant larger commercial clients that don't shop based only on the lowest price and that pay their bills on time. "I couldn't do that at first, but I wanted to make sure I was moving in that direction," Ken said.

At the end of six months, Ken sat down with his wife to decide whether JMG Security Systems was reaching its goals. "If yes, we would go forward; if no, then we wouldn't sink more money into it. We'd be smart enough to look for something else," Ken said. The Jacobses gave their venture the go-ahead, but Ken acknowledged that if the company hadn't been moving in the right direction, closing it would have been a tough decision. After the first year, Ken never questioned JMG Security Systems' viability. He deliberately pursued and won well-known accounts, such as Nordstrom department stores; Edison International Field, the baseball stadium of the Anaheim Angels; Knott's Berry Farm; and The Home Depot stores throughout Southern California. "Once you have one of these plums, no one questions your credibility," Ken said. "I have outlasted all my major national competitors."

51. NEVER STOP LEARNING

Classes, seminars, books, and audiotapes on business
management are invaluable aids in launching a business.

■ ■ ■

Ron Schmitz grew up on a farm, but he was a born carpenter. The first purchase he ever made, at the age of 16, was a table saw. Ron decided college would bore him; however, he did attend two years of trade school in carpentry before he got the opportunity to buy a run-down cabinet shop in Sauk Rapids, Minnesota, in January 1975. He was 23 years old. Shortly after he took over, he had to fire the man who was to show him how to run the business.

That initial year, Ron's Cabinets, Inc., had revenues of $80,000 and two employees. Ron took care of the customers, while his wife, Dianne, handled the finances. Although Ron knew the technical side of cabinet making, he knew little about business. He didn't have experience with taxes, personnel, business management, or marketing. "I should have gotten some formal education in business before buying [the company]," Ron said. In fact, his lack of business knowledge almost cost him the business. "In the first two years, it wasn't a question about profitability," Ron said. "I would do anything just to break even so we didn't lose the place."

The turning point was an advertisement that came in the mail for a series of seminars on business management. Ron and Dianne went to the introduction to get a free dinner. They couldn't take the time and money away from the business to attend such a long, expensive course, but Ron bought the audiotapes, which covered much of the same information. "That turned me around; I learned so much," he said. "I would listen to tapes on the road to jobs. I listened to them 10, 20 times."

After that, Ron signed up for every short course and seminar he could find on business topics. He attended thousands of them over the years. Because he couldn't take a semester off from running the business, Ron concentrated on one-hour, three-hour, and one-day workshops. Also, he sought out successful businesspeople and asked endless questions. "They usually were willing to share information," Ron said. He found to be most valuable tapes by Brian Tracy and Zig Ziglar and seminars in insurance, personnel issues, taxes, marketing, and basic how-tos of running a business. Ron's informal yet unrelenting education paid off. By 1979, Ron's Cabinets had grown so much, it moved into a larger building. Ron invested in new technology, such as computer-aided design and engineering. He developed a highly integrated production and management team. The company won awards for its quality.

Finally, in 1997, when Ron's Cabinet's sales topped $7 million, Ron sold the company. His brother's death from a heart attack at age 47 a short time earlier had been a wake-up call for Ron. He had many other endeavors he wanted to pursue; none of them was in business. In addition, the timing was right, Ron said. Interest rates were low, potential buyers were plentiful, and businesses sell best when they're doing well. "Besides, the business was growing, but I didn't want to take it to the next level," Ron said. He did, however, continue to attend seminars and listen to business tapes until the day he sold the company. "Over the years, I found that people who don't need the information that much are always [at the seminars], and those who need it most aren't," Ron said. "Always continue your education as long as you want to succeed in business."

52. CLIENTS KNOW BEST

A successful business must focus on what clients want
rather than on what the owner thinks they should have.

■ ■ ■

After three decades working in various businesses, Jim Collison became the founding executive director of a statewide employers' group in Iowa in the 1970s. In 1981, he acquired the organization by assuming its $30,000 in debts. Jim then changed it to a for-profit business and changed the name to Independent Small Business Employers of America, Inc. (Later, he renamed it Employers of America—EofA.)

Organizations, whether nonprofit or for-profit, don't fall into debt by accident. "It took me years to overcome my compulsion to sell what I knew with certainty that bosses needed and concentrate on what they wanted," Jim said. "The worst reason to invest time, money, and energy into a business is because you are in love with the concept or the product or the activity. Unless enough potential customers or clients like what you offer well enough to pay for it, your business is doomed."

The association started as a lobbyist for employer issues, working on political issues with lawmakers. "Frankly, that's not what most employers, managers, and supervisors cared about," Jim said. "Besides, the National Federation of Independent Business and U.S. Chamber of Commerce dominated the political arena like Wal-Mart dominates retailing." EofA members consistently called Jim in his Mason City, Iowa, office for advice and guidance on employee-related problems. Finally, the light dawned, and Jim dropped the lobbying. "We put our energy into helping bosses deal with what they wanted most: to avoid headaches and to achieve more when dealing with employees."

Business associations have many opportunities to sell products and services on behalf of other companies. In fact, these groups must have such sales because they can't live on members' dues alone. Jim received several offers a month for a 1 percent to 10 percent royalty or fee if he would promote to EofA members such items as insurance, credit cards, long-distance telephone service, computer software, overnight shipping services, bill-collection services, and equipment leases. However, Jim would not accept any of these items unless his members strongly indicated they wanted it through surveys in the group's monthly newsletter, "Smart Workplace Practices." He also asked visitors to EofA's Web site for comments, experiences, and ideas. Because of members' interest, EofA did offer group health insurance, but few other products and services. "A consultant was trying to interest me in doing a story in the newsletter about why employers need to offer their employees the new benefit he is marketing. I told him, 'I agree that employers and their employees need what you have, but I have strong doubts that they want it.'"

Jim used members' comments to guide many of his business decisions. "For years, we offered members an employee handbook writing service," Jim said. "But custom-written employee handbooks were expensive, and few employers wanted to pay the kind of fee that was needed for a well-written handbook." When Jim would give a $2,000 or $3,000 quote for a handbook, many employers would gasp and say something like, "I was thinking more like $200." So, finally, he put together *The Complete Employee Handbook Made Easy,* with 300 pages of 101 policy topics, including 240 sample policies.

Through continual tweaking, Jim built EofA to more than a thousand members in 40 states. In addition to the handbook and monthly newsletter, Jim and his staff of 12 provided telephone and fax-back advice and coaching on employment-related issues. "I recommend you do some kind of market survey before you plunge headlong into your business with all your money or the money of friends and relatives," Jim said. "And continue to survey your market as long as you're in business."

53. NO INSTANT SUCCESSES

Many business owners work years without
taking money out of their businesses.

■ ■ ■

Rowena Fullinwider loved to make almond pound cakes, jams, and jellies for holiday gifts for friends or to raise money for local charities. Soon her foods were so popular that people encouraged her to start her own business. "I had no financial background, no marketing or sales experience, limited finances, and no business credit," Rowena said. "In addition, I had no manufacturing or equipment experience, and the only customers were church bazaars, charities, and a few store owners who loved the product."

Nevertheless, Rowena did extensive planning, renovated an old warehouse for a gourmet manufacturing plant, and opened Rowena's, Inc., in Norfolk, Virginia, in 1983. She had one full-time employee and a lot of nerve. "God was my copilot," she said. "I decided at the beginning that I did not have the knowledge to go it alone. Therefore, after analyzing problems, I frequently gave them up to Him."

To survive during the start-up period, Rowena worked an evening job as chemist at a local hospital for more than six years while getting the company on its feet. She did not draw any salary from Rowena's, Inc., for four years so she could make sure her employees were paid. "I was determined to survive," she said. "I had this thing going, and I couldn't just walk away. "I worked all the time," Rowena said. "I gave up community work. I stopped sewing. I stopped cooking. I had to let many things slide."

Because she was working two jobs, Rowena depended on her employees to share her business vision and help grow the company. She made sure the employees understood company costs and the need for efficiency. "We instituted time, motion process, and raw material studies of all products to find [their] true cost," she said. "We then set in place cost reduction procedures, in some cases dropping the product if it could not be produced and delivered to the customer profitably." However, Rowena wouldn't delegate certain management jobs. Although she hired a plant manager with an MBA in finance, she actively participated in all financial decisions. Also, she took a college accounting class so she could understand her financial statements. When her manager left after two years, she was able to run the company on her own.

"I grew this business without debt," she said. "I expanded my line of credit each year to cover growth, but I paid it off early each year, which pleased my banker. I undertook an aggressive reading program, scanning the literature for applicability to my business and sharing valuable information with the appropriate team members," Rowena said. She networked continuously in the community and her industry to gain more knowledge. She helped found the Food and Libation Association of Virginia to provide food manufacturers like Rowena with networking, information, and shared advertising opportunities.

Gradually, over the years, Rowena was able to cut back her hours at the hospital until she finally quit. Rowena's, Inc., eventually moved into an 8,000-square-foot warehouse with a factory and small retail store. Sixteen full-time and 45 seasonal employees filled orders within 48 hours. The products were sold mostly through 3,000 gourmet stores and gift shops and to gift basket manufacturers. Although people thinking about going into business shouldn't underestimate the amount of work and sacrifice ahead, that shouldn't stop them, Rowena said. "When you want to go into business, you have a choice: gather all your information and go forward or do nothing," she said. "My advice is just move forward."

54.

IN SEARCH OF
THE IDEAL CUSTOMER

Start-up companies often work with less than ideal
customers before winning lucrative accounts.

■ ■ ■

After graduating from high school, Dan Zettler worked for a machine shop, where he invested hundreds of hours of his own time to master computer-operated machines that could create tiny parts for watches and other products. That preparation paid off. When Dan was just 22 years old, one of the machine shop's customers asked him to create a prototype for an electronic component. In 1988, Dan left the shop to start Zet-Tek to manufacture electronic contacts and medical components in Anaheim, California.

"At first, we dealt with little companies because that was our only choice," Dan said. "We wanted big companies, but their buyers didn't want to take the risk to hire us." Unfortunately, some of these small firms were cash poor. They paid their bills 90 days or 120 days past due. A couple of them went bankrupt, owing Zet-Tek money. "We lost $1,500 or so, which was a lot in those days," Dan said. "That might be our profit for the month. I couldn't take a paycheck when that happened."

Dan tried early in his company's history to get a contract with an international office equipment manufacturer. "I would have done anything to get in the door at that company," he said. But the buyer told him that the company was reducing its vendor list in his category from 22 companies to five. A few entrepreneurs start with one or more large corporate contracts, but most, like Dan, scramble to attract larger, more financially stable accounts. It can take years of persistence in contacting corporate buyers and hard work at building the kind of reputation a big company wants in its suppliers. It helps if the start-up has a unique product or service that the large corporation cannot or does not want to provide for itself. It also helps if the entrepreneur researches extensively the corporation he's targeting in order to contact the right people, understand the company's procedures, and ferret out the company's specific needs.

From the beginning, Zet-Tek was known for quality and precision; however, the recession of the early 1990s made it difficult for Dan to attract the bigger accounts he wanted in order to grow Zet-Tek. He had to build his track record through smaller contracts first. Fortunately for Dan, purchasing managers frequently moved from job to job in his industry. Buyers for existing Zet-Tek clients continually took similar jobs at other companies in the area. When they did, they usually gave Dan contracts with the new companies because of the quality work he did for them previously. Zet-Tek's quality workmanship, relationship building, persistence, and staying power through tough economic times slowly paid off. Many of Zet-Tek's competitors went out of business or were sold during this period. "It took six years to prove ourselves this way," Dan said.

Dan also found that it didn't pay to pursue an endless stream of new corporate accounts at the expense of his existing customers. As Zet-Tek grew to ship $500,000 in finished parts each month, Dan was careful to service established customers' needs first. "We have told some people that we're not accepting new customers because we're maxed out at this factory," Dan said. However, he was also able to cut off business relationships with those late-paying customers who hurt Zet-Tek's finances. This way, he said, his customer base became more lucrative over time. This growth strategy finally brought Dan the ultimate compliment: The international manufacturer whose business he would have died to acquire in 1988 invited him to become one of its vendors.

55.   RECOVERING FROM A MOVE

A service business that relies on local clients will have a difficult
time surviving a move to a new geographic market.

■ ■ ■

Organizational psychologist Donna Genett worked for years consulting and coaching business executives. However, the president of GenCorp Consulting, a national training and development firm headquartered in Seattle, Washington, found herself almost having to start her business from scratch when she moved her home to Huntington Beach, California, in 2000. It wasn't apparent at the time, but an economic slowdown made that year a bad time to move. The U.S. economy softened and finally fell into a mild recession, and many companies were shedding outside service contracts, which is typical during weak economies. It didn't help GenCorp Consulting that Donna had to add her travel expenses to her consulting fees. Donna had built her business through word-of-mouth marketing from one client to another. However, this strategy was less effective long distance when the existing customer base was in a different geographic region. "Once you build a practice, people in that area know you, but when you move to a new location you no longer have that network," she said.

A move can be good for a young business. It represents growth and vitality. It can provide an opportunity to clear away products or services that are least profitable or passe. But a move can be disastrous if it erodes your customer base. Some business owners take aggressive marketing action, sending announcements and e-mails about the move. They pay to keep their old phone number for a year with a recorded notice about the company's new phone number and address. One important reason for this step is that telephone directories with Yellow Pages advertising stay in homes and offices at least a year. Some people hang on to them longer.

These marketing efforts were less effective for Donna because the economy was hurting her business as much as the move and word-of-mouth marketing wasn't working long distance. "I tried networking, cold calling, all the traditional ways of contacting businesses, but executives were trying to save their businesses. They weren't hiring consultants," Donna said. So she took the opportunity to reposition her consulting service to focus on the problems executives have delegating responsibilities to others. She previously had encountered this issue repeatedly when coaching executives. "Every executive came to me with different symptoms, but the problem was always the same: they could delegate," she said. "There's no place to learn these skills, and everyone said my advice was so helpful I should write a book about it."

So she did, during the slow period following her move. *If You Want It Done Right, You Don't Have to Do It Yourself* was published in 2003 and complements her seminars, speeches, CDs, and workbooks. "I used the book as my entry ticket," she said. "The timing was perfect, because the book was published right as the economy was starting to build. So executives were looking at productivity without immediately adding jobs. To do that, they needed to delegate."

56. CUSTOMER NIGHTMARES

Your troubles don't necessarily end when
you get your first customers.

■ ■ ■

Ted Hunter's family had worked in construction for three genera-
tions, but 1989 seemed like a good time for Ted to switch from building
real estate to building computers. Ted launched Downtime, Inc., in Brun-
swick, Maine, to specialize in developing and servicing computer networks for companies of all sizes. While real estate and computers seem
very different, "the basic principles apply to all businesses," Ted said.

The late 1980s and early 1990s weren't good times for start-ups in
many industries. The economy dragged, and business capital was scarce.
Few companies were building, but neither were they buying computer networks. "My first three clients were absolute disasters," Ted said. One was
a consignment store that closed suddenly. The owner skipped town without
paying Ted. The second was an accountant who paid his bill slowly over
several years. The third was a comic book store that went bankrupt. Ted
was never paid for this job either. "And this was after doing all the research
and figuring how to pay the bills," Ted said.

Such stories aren't unusual. Even with the best-laid plans and market
research, new businesses have a tough time attracting their first customers
or clients. Most accept less than ideal assignments to start. Some don't ad-
equately check the creditworthiness of these first accounts, but even if they
do, things can go wrong. Ted did not allow his initial clients to ruin his
business or his attitude. He had enough resources to carry him three years,
if necessary, without drawing a paycheck. He learned the necessity of controlling costs from his grandfather, who kept the cost estimate for every
construction job he ever bid. Ted broadened Downtime's base to several
industries and types of customers. Construction was an important source
of clients initially, but Ted eventually reduced it to less than 8 percent of
his business. Ted moved to attract more shipping and transportation clients. Downtime, builder of computer networks and seller of components,
networked the computers of ten Wal-Mart stores. But end users weren't
Downtime's only market. The company also was a subcontractor for as-

sembly houses that had contracts with major manufacturers to assemble and install networks. "We put together the computer system and the software and make the customized software work," Ted said.

Customers always come and go—sometimes without paying—no matter how old or sophisticated a company is. For example, Downtime had a contract with one of the largest computer manufacturers to service computers under warranty. That manufacturer then signed a nationwide repair deal with a large consumer electronic retail chain. Such fickleness is why small companies need a mix of customers, products, and services.

It is also important to keep in close contact with clients, said Ted, who continually visited clients to stay in touch with their needs and occasionally worked at one of their sites, perhaps manning the customer service phone line for a day. "I didn't buy a thousand computers from them, so I wasn't at the top of their minds; I had to stay in their faces," he explained. "I gave them a day of my time free, and it put me in touch with the field." This kind of handholding is a lot of work, but it probably ensures that you won't be surprised if the client goes bankrupt.

57. GET THE GOODS ONTO THE SHELVES

A young company must gain full distribution for its products.

■ ■ ■

After graduating from college, Toxey Haas accepted a job as production manager for a food company. However, a steady, corporate career wasn't Toxey's long-term plan. A hunter since childhood in Mississippi, he wanted to develop a better camouflage pattern for hunters' clothing. In 1986, 26-year-old Toxey created Haas Outdoors, Inc., in West Point, Mississippi, copyrighted his camouflage patterns, and trademarked the name Mossy Oak. Haas Outdoors contracted with a clothing manufacturer to make high-quality hunting apparel, using Toxey's designs. Toxey's original strategy was to be the Ralph Lauren of hunting clothes, so he carefully limited distribution of his products, which included gloves, pants, jackets, caps, and boots. He also limited the retailers that could stock Mossy Oak, allowing them to carry the clothing exclusively in their geographic areas. "We were so selective with where Mossy Oak was sold that we hurt ourselves," Toxey said. "We built tremendous consumer demand, but people complained that they couldn't find our products."

One reason companies limit distribution is to ensure quality. But Haas Outdoors could produce larger quantities without compromising quality, so the exclusive strategy unnecessarily limited company growth. "The bottom line for the retailer is that it doesn't need an exclusive territory if we can maintain consumer demand coming into the store," Toxey said. Haas Outdoors changed its strategy to make Mossy Oak more like Nike, available wherever sporting goods were sold. "Once your brand is national in scope, quality is not an issue if you have a truly unique product," Toxey said.

A manufacturer must accept its role in attracting sales when distributors and retailers stock its products. Making a quality product is key, but not the only responsibility. The manufacturer must create demand through advertising and provide marketing materials such as brochures the distributor can show its retail clients, as well as in-store displays the retailer can use. The manufacturer also must value the products at a price consumers will pay, which requires calculation of markups for distributors and retailers. The manufacturer may need to include incentives for the distributors' sales forces. After the products get into the stores, it is the manufacturer's responsibility to fill all orders quickly and provide good customer service or, for some products, technical support.

Haas Outdoors' shift toward wider distribution brought its own challenges. For example, hunting was extremely popular in West Virginia, but Mossy Oak sales were low in that state. Therefore, Haas Outdoors opened a factory store in West Virginia that charged regular retail prices, but stocked everything in the Mossy Oak line. "We did 20 times more business through that one store than we previously sold through wholesale in the entire state," Toxey said. "In addition, the store created great exposure for us. That's a big tourist area, so people bought our clothing, then went home and asked their local sporting goods stores for more Mossy Oak products." The exposure also brought greater sales for other retailers that stocked the Mossy Oak line.

Haas Outdoors' strategy broadened even more for greater distribution. The company created a retailing division to develop specialty shopping malls for all types of outdoor sporting products. Another division created a line of casual nonhunting sportswear called Mossy Oak Companions. A third division produced the company's own television commercials and advertising. "Everything we did fit in with outdoor sports," Toxey said. Haas Outdoors was no longer the simple camouflage clothier Toxey envisioned right out of college. "This rapid horizontal integration brought back-to-back years of 50 percent-plus growth," he said.

58. WHO'S NEXT?

Succession planning is essential to save your company if
a key executive dies suddenly or suffers debilitating injury.

■ ■ ■

Connie Kostrzewa was a preschool teacher in 1982 when her father, Val Kostrzewa, told her that he planned to buy a bankrupt Saginaw, Michigan, machinery company with eight employees. Connie grew up in manufacturing—her dad and grandfather started a company in their garage when she was a child—but she had gone into teaching to assert her independence. Connie was interested in the new venture, however. She sat in on planning meetings and started taking college business classes. Val bought Miles Machinery with his two brothers and renamed it K-Miles Co. Val was the only one actively involved in running the company when he died 11 months later. The company was to go through some wrenching problems because of the sudden loss of leadership. The company faced continued financial insecurity and economic volatility because it hadn't planned for such a possibility. Also, it lacked key-man life insurance, which is designed to help companies pay inheritance taxes and other costs when an integral employee dies. "There was a desperate need for someone to step in and run the company because of all the bank loans taken out to buy the company," Connie said. She already was working at the company during summer break. Following her father's death, she took a leave of absence from teaching and finally made her commitment to the company permanent.

Shortly before Val's death, Dale Wright, a long-time business associate, merged his engineering firm with K-Miles to create Wright-K Technology. Dale helped the new special-order machinery manufacturer grow to 37 employees. Then, nine months after Val's death, Dale died. This time, Wright-K had key-man life insurance; however, the company lacked a succession plan and had to totally reorganize its internal operations and corporate goals. The family persuaded another long-time Kostrzewa business associate, Dick DeYoung, to come out of retirement to become president. They asked Robert Floeter, who had been a salesman for Val for 31 years, to become sales manager. Eleven months later, Dick became seriously ill and had to resign. Again, the company—already losing money—had to reorganize.

Any one of these losses could have sunk Wright-K. Inheritance taxes alone put many companies out of business when an owner dies. However, a succession plan is more than just replacing the owner. Its goal is to strengthen the company to meet its needs three to five years down the line. The plan helps a company grow, protects it from loss of key employees, and prepares for the inevitable change that follows such loss. Ideally, a business owner thinks about passing on the business when starting the company. Begin your planning by developing clear goals and objectives for yourself and your company. Predict potential changes in your industry and individual business; then identify the skills and organizational structure your company will need to meet those changes. Start relinquishing duties to others by training existing employees to fill future needs or by hiring people who can fill these needs. Never assume your children have the talents or interest to take over the business.

In the 1985 reorganization, Robert Floeter became chief executive officer, and John Sivey, who had just merged his manufacturing firm into Wright-K, became vice president. Connie became secretary/treasurer. This time, the company funded key-man insurance policies and set up stock buy-sell agreements. Wright-K became a specialist in designing, building, and rebuilding machinery by special order. However, employees never stopped training and upgrading their skills. They just never knew when they might be called on to assume some leadership role.

PART 5

HELPING HANDS

■ ■ ■

Every new business owner needs help. Even the one-person home-based operation can accomplish more at greater speed and with less hassle with assistance. Others have been where you are now. You'll be astounded how helpful they are willing to be if you let them know you need and value their advice.

You really know your business is on its way when you start tapping the help of outside experts. (Just remember, you own the place; don't abdicate that role to any expert.) However, the real challenge begins when you hire help. Communication is key when you take on the role of employer along with business owner. You must relate your needs and expectations to job applicants as well as employees. They will never do the job right if you don't explain it first. Employees who know the rules of the game are likely to follow them. Those who are rewarded for meeting your goals are likely to exceed them.

But it all begins with you. You define the job descriptions. You set the rules. You establish the goals. You create the rewards. The catch is that new business owners, especially those who chafed at the rules in former corporate jobs, really hate to create the needed structure.

59. REWARD YOUR WORKERS

If you share your success with key employees, they will exceed
your expectations and contribute to even greater success.

■ ■ ■

Bob Basham and Chris Sullivan thought they might own a couple of
restaurants in the Tampa, Florida, area when they first set up Multi-Venture
Partners, Inc., in 1987. They wanted a casual atmosphere and a steak-based
menu, so they chose an Australian theme and opened Outback Steakhouse.
Within three years, that became the name of the whole corporation, which
grew to almost a thousand restaurants under seven different names in 15
years. But from the beginning, Bob and Chris decided they would give a
piece of ownership to key people in order to attract the best workers and
encourage outstanding performance.

This policy applied not just to corporate directors but also to all general managers, who were required to purchase an interest, usually 10 percent, for $25,000 in the restaurants they ran. "You have to incentivize
people early on," Bob explained. A manager "invests his hard-earned
money and he gets cash flow distribution and at the end of his five-year
contract he has equity." This arrangement wasn't a gift. Outback demanded quality performance in finances and service. As part of the reward
structure, if a manager performed well, he could open more restaurants.

The incentives worked. Managers with a stake in their restaurants usually outperformed Outback's expectations. Bob told of one manager who
opened more than 50 restaurants in a market that the company thought
would support 10 to 12 units. This approach contributed to the phenomenal
growth of Outback Steakhouse, Bob said. The company was the fastest
growing, nonfranchise, full-service restaurant chain in U.S. history, reaching 100 units in the first five years. The company had more than 60,000
employees in 22 countries by 2004. That growth wasn't the goal, Bob said.
"We always wanted to take care of customers one at a time, build restaurants one at a time. It's a mistake to worry about your hundredth restaurant
when you have just one."

Outback Steakhouse did build one restaurant at a time, but at an incredible pace, by sharing equity with managers. It made the same equity offer to managers of its other concepts: Carrabba Italian Grills, Fleming Prime Steakhouse and Wine Bar, Roy's Hawaiian Cuisine, Lee Roy Selmon's (Southern "comfort recipes"), Bonefish Grills (seafood), and Cheeseburger in Paradise. "I'm surprised more companies don't use this approach. A lot of business owners don't share their success," Bob said. "What happens is that the owner thinks the incentivized managers are making too much money, maybe more than the owner. At Outback we took the approach that if the manager was making money, then we were making money. If they were off the charts, great. If they were making more than Chris and I made, well, we were still making more than we would without them." Some other companies have offered such incentives, and then withdrawn them when employees were successful, Bob said. "That's not right. You should stick to your plan. Share success and not change deals on employees."

60.   ASK FOR OUTSIDE HELP

Don't reinvent the wheel when many individuals and groups are
willing to help guild your business start-up and growth.

■ ■ ■

Twin sisters Lauri and Carol Raymond started making and distributing a salad dressing, sauce, and marinade in 1988 not because they were great cooks, but because they didn't have time to be great cooks and figured other people faced the same dilemma. They called the product SASS, meaning "season all stuff sauce," to convey its versatility. The company, Sisters & Brothers, Inc., started gaining a following among Austin, Texas, health food stores and upscale markets because SASS used fresh ingredients and no additives or artificial preservatives. The company created such flavors as Sesame-Garlic, Tomato-Basil, Rancho-Grande, and Lemon-Song. Soon supermarkets wanted SASS too.

During the early years, Lauri, who was company president, had lots of questions about all aspects of running a business, but she didn't ask them. "I think I was too embarrassed to admit I didn't know everything, and so our company spent a lot of time reinventing the wheel," she said. "Even though my sister and I had each other, our experience was so similar (we ARE twins) that we really needed some outside input in the system."

Many fledgling business owners share Lauri's reluctance, unaware of the free and low-cost resources for small businesses. Most veteran business owners gladly share their hard-earned wisdom, remembering how hard it is to get over the start-up hump. Even the smallest business should consult with an accountant and attorney, who willingly steer new clients through the start-up shoals in the expectation of helping create larger, more successful clients. Every owner should set up a separate business bank account and start cultivating a relationship with a banker, who also helps companies grow in order to grow his own institution. In addition, nonprofit business groups, trade associations, colleges, and government agencies offer meetings, classes, publications, business counseling, and Web sites to help small-business owners. "We thought we were too busy to join small-business groups or women's business groups," Lauri recalled, "but it turned out that talking to others would have been such a time-saver."

Carol moved to Santa Fe, New Mexico, in 1994, leaving Lauri to run all the day-to-day operations of Sisters & Brothers, which by that time had incorporated. Lauri continued to add new products and in 1997, Sesame-Garlic SASS won first place at the New York Fancy Food and Confections Show. In 2001, Sisters & Brothers acquired a friendly local competitor, Martin Brothers Fresh Dressings, building the product line to 16 dressings and three dips.

"I finally got involved in several local networks for small businesses, environmentally and socially conscious businesses, women-owned business, even food businesses," Lauri said. "It was so energizing, refreshing, educational, and fun to connect with others who shared the same interests and had dealt with the same problems." She also joined The Alternative Board (TAB), which brings up to 12 business executives together in a group that meets monthly with a certified facilitator to share problems and advice. Similar organizations include TEC (formerly The Executive Committee), Renaissance Executive Forums, and BBL (Beyond Bottom Line) Forums. "Since I was my own boss, it also helped to have a network to which I was accountable," Lauri said. "It kept me moving forward."

61. DELEGATE TO GROW

Assigning employees to routine tasks helps them learn and
frees you to spend more time growing the business.

■ ■ ■

As a child, Richard Yobs sold eggs door to door with his father.
"Never work for anyone else if you can help it," the senior Yobs advised
during their travels. That advice planted a seed in Richard's mind that took
root when he accepted a job as manager of a paint store when he was in his
early 20s. "From the day I went into that job, I thought I could own my own
store someday if things went right," Richard said. His boss was rarely at
the store, so Richard learned every aspect of paint retailing "except signing
the paychecks." It was invaluable experience. "Too many people go into
business without taking the time to learn how first," he said. After five
years of managing and learning on the job, Richard opened Painten Place
in Denville, New Jersey, in 1971. The retail paint and wall covering store
had hundreds of commercial accounts as well as individual customers.
Richard supplied expertise and information even professional painters
didn't have.

In the beginning, Richard did it all. "I needed to learn how to delegate
authority, not just go through the motions," Richard said. "You must delegate day-to-day jobs, so you can spend more time growing your business,
buying better, and networking." The cost to a business is monumental,
sometimes fatal, if the entrepreneur spends too much time on routine tasks
that anyone can do and never gets around to the strategic planning and
high-level work that only the owner can do. "Oh, I'd give someone the
keys and let him open or close, but I never gave anyone the authority to
make a decision so I could get out to make important sales calls," Richard
said. "Then, as soon as I left, the store would get busy, and I'd have to run
back and make decisions." A business owner has only so much time. Richard could spend all his time in the store doing a $6-an-hour clerk's job,
or he could hire someone else to do that job and devote his time to going
out to customers' locations and selling. "On the road, I was worth $1,000
an hour," he said.

Few entrepreneurs know instinctively how to delegate. Even fewer want to. They try to do everything, usually for one of two reasons. They think they can't afford help, or they think no one can do the job as well as they can. "If you allow people to make decisions, they will," Richard said. "They are going to make mistakes because we all do, but then they learn and do better the next time." Getting over his own do-it-all syndrome took extreme self-discipline, Richard said. First, he had to hire and train people to work in the store and service the customers the way he wanted it done. "Then I had to say, 'Bye, I'm going out on the road; you'll have to do it without me,'" he said. "It took a couple of years for me to get comfortable leaving." Richard eventually developed two employees whom he could trust with the whole operation. He felt comfortable allowing the others to fill in for brief periods or in specific jobs. "Delegation is the only way a company can grow," Richard said. "The business gets too big for the owner to do it all."

62. THE SEARCH FOR GOOD WORKERS

It is difficult for small businesses to find
and keep production workers.

■ ■ ■

Anne Grimes, a one-time deli manager for a large supermarket, owned a small bake shop in Ayden, North Carolina. Customers often asked for dumplings to put in their chicken recipes, but Anne always told them she didn't make dumplings—until one persistent customer wore her down. Anne dumped some ingredients into a mixer, rolled out the dough, and froze four boxes of dumplings. The customer was so delighted with the product that word spread that Anne made the most delicious dumplings, which were convenient because they were frozen. Anne and her husband, Bryan, bought a pastry-making machine and converted their home carport into a dumpling factory in 1981. They called their side venture Harvest Time Foods. Sales exploded so rapidly, first to grocery stores and then to warehouses that supplied grocery chains, that Anne closed the bakery and

Bryan quit his job as manager of a hospital parking lot. Their son, Bryan III, was recruited to help with distribution. Within a year, the Grimeses moved Harvest Time Foods into a commercial building, and three years later, they bought a larger building. When they moved again, they converted the former factory into a youth center and donated it to a church.

Despite its success, the company always had difficulty hiring and keeping enough production workers. These jobs did not demand a high level of education, but required people who understood the importance of production quotas and quality products. "Although no training was needed for our production jobs, we preferred high school graduates with good work ethics," Anne said. The Grimeses are not alone. Many fast-growing start-up businesses have difficulty finding workers. Then, after the expense of training new hires, the companies have difficulty keeping them. Small businesses usually are at a disadvantage when it comes to pay rates, fringe benefits, and opportunities for advancement within the company. Companies like Harvest Time Foods, trying to fill entry-level jobs, struggle more. In rural areas and times of low unemployment, the problem is worse.

Anne thought internship and apprenticeship programs at local schools and colleges might have helped Harvest Time Foods solve its problem. The company could have worked with the schools in its area to create a combination of classroom education and on-the-job experience. Some companies offer employees cash rewards for helping recruit new employees. Others send recruiters to trade shows, community fairs, and even parks on sunny weekend afternoons. Harvest Time Foods resorted to mechanical help. Originally, Harvest Time Foods' workers mixed, rolled, and cut pastry dough into dumplings. They then hand-packed the completed product and wrapped the boxes. The Grimeses found machinery to do all that work, including layering the dumplings in boxes without damaging them. Over a three-year period, the company's staffing needs declined from 55 jobs to eight with triple the production capacity. However, Harvest Time Foods did not lay off workers. Because the automation process was accomplished over several years, the company brought in temporary workers whenever permanent employees left. Son B.G. became company president in 1996. "By reducing our workforce by automation, we could offer higher wages to the workers we kept," Anne said.

63. HIRE THE BEST

Many business start-ups try to save money by hiring
cheap labor. It pays to hire the best-quality personnel.

■   ■   ■

Scott Sorensen had just graduated from college when he stepped in
to save the family moving company in 1977. His mother had kept Sorensen
Moving & Storage afloat since his father's death, but Melbourne, Florida,
was in a prolonged recession that threatened to sink the agent for Allied
Van Lines. "Many times, because of budgetary constraints, new business
owners—and owners of established businesses, for that matter—try to get
by hiring cheap," Scott said. "I have learned from experience that it pays
to hire the best people you can because your business is only as good as the
team members associated with you." Scott learned to define the overall
team his company needed, to carefully craft job descriptions for the individuals who made up that team, and to clarify some intangibles that pull
the two together. Taking time to clarify these work goals helps business
owners know what they're looking for when hiring. It also attracts the right
employees.

Scott started with the big picture: "The best team is one that can work
together to meet individual objectives and company goals at the same
time," he said. To build that team, it helps to develop objective, job-related
selection criteria. If the worker must be able to type, don't hire someone
who can't. If the job requires selling experience, don't hire someone who
has none. In his search for the best managers, Scott often recruited from
other industries. For the best sales and marketing people, he recruited from
competitors. He also looked for qualifications not found on any résumé. "I
looked for attitude; people who could be good team players within the organization; for good values away from work; and for people who could do
more than just the jobs they were being hired for," he explained.

Scott wanted people with multiple work capabilities because he
believed in hiring from within. He also wanted workers eager for greater
responsibilities. In fact, the company had at least 15 managers who
worked their way up through the ranks. One former employee was so
eager for greater responsibility, however, that he left to start his own mov-

ing company in another market. Scott acknowledged that his hires weren't always perfect. "We'd like to hire all nines and tens, of course, but sometimes a seven or eight was the best we can find," he said. "They were outstanding in one area, but weak in another. So we had to match their strengths with our jobs." That's a juggling act that many inexperienced business owners fail to appreciate. Scott became good enough at finding and keeping the right staffing combination that he was able to expand beyond residential and business moves into additional services, such as transporting high-tech equipment. He also opened a separate Allied Van Lines franchise in Orlando, Florida, in 1994, using managers from the Melbourne company to run it. He did the same in opening a self-storage company. "I always hope to promote from within," he said. "The higher caliber the personnel you have on your team, the more you put yourself in a position to be successful."

64. YOU CAN'T ASK THAT!

Learn to find the right employees without asking legally prohibited questions.

■ ■ ■

Nancy Friedman was so angered by the rude way her insurance broker's employees treated her on the phone that she cancelled all her policies. The stunned broker asked Nancy to come in and talk with his employees about proper phone etiquette. She certainly was familiar with the topic. She handled customer relations for her husband's business, Weatherline, Inc., a telephone weather report service in St. Louis, Missouri. That presentation in 1982 was the start of Telephone Doctor, a company that trains businesspeople worldwide in proper phone manners through seminars and videotapes. However, if Telephone Doctor was going to be credible, employees had to practice what Nancy preached. "It was so hard to hire the right people because there were so many questions employers couldn't ask job applicants," Nancy said.

Many questions once common in a job interview have been made illegal by federal and state laws prohibiting job discrimination based on

ethnicity, sex, age, religion, or disability. Even some questions job inter-
viewers used to ask to put applicants at ease, such as do you have children
or are you married, are off limits. For example, you can't ask job applicants whether they have diseases that aren't job related. You can't question whether they have ever been arrested. (You can, however, determine
whether they have ever been convicted of a felony.) You can't ask whether
they belong to certain clubs (which might indicate religion or ethnicity)
or even whether they are male or female.

The key to avoiding legal problems is to focus the interview on job requirements and company policies. For instance, you can describe the work
that is part of a job and ask whether the applicant can do it. If it's a warehouse job, can the applicant lift 50-pound boxes? If it's a delivery job, does
the applicant have a valid driver's license, and can he drive 200 miles a
day, five days a week? A disabled person might be able to do a job with
some accommodation that you are required to provide. For example, a person may be a whiz-bang typist, but need wheelchair access to the building.

But just as significant as avoiding illegal questions is finding the right
questions to weed out applicants who are poorly suited for particular jobs.
The last thing Telephone Doctor needed was someone who was rude on
the phone, for example. "I needed people who could think on their feet.
They needed to be knowledgeable, friendly," Nancy said. "We gave applicants a simple quiz. What newspapers do you read? Who is the vice president of the United States? Questions like that. I wouldn't hire someone
who didn't know the vice president."

Each employer should carefully craft some questions that get to the
heart of the job being filled. For example, to assess leadership skills, you
might ask how the applicant would discipline an errant worker. However,
word it in such a way that you can determine whether the applicant has any
experience. Say, for instance, "Tell me about a time when you had to discipline an employee." Or describe a situation that your workers really encounter in their jobs, and ask the applicant to role-play a solution. Don't
rely on interviews alone, however. Too many people have taken seminars
in how to ace a job interview. Always check references and, if appropriate,
give a skills test. Nancy's employees were friendly, helpful, and—you
heard in their voices—smiling. They never said, "I don't know" without
adding "but I'll find out for you." All of these were skills that Nancy taught
employees at other corporations, so, naturally, they were part of the job description at Telephone Doctor.

65. COMPLEMENT YOURSELF

Hire people with skills different than yours that
supply needed expertise in running a business.

■ ■ ■

Pam Lontos was so good at selling radio advertising for her broadcast employer that her boss wanted to make her the general manager of one of the company's radio stations. But Pam knew her skills and interests lay in selling and training others to sell, not in doing budgets and paperwork. So, in 1981, Pam started Lontos Sales & Motivation, a consulting, training, and seminar firm in Dallas, Texas. It later moved to Orlando, Florida, along with Pam's other company, PR/PR. "I would hire people just like myself," said Pam, an effervescent personality who once had her own television program. "I found that other business owners tended to do the same thing. Creative people hire creative people. "So I had all creative people in my office, and no one balanced the checkbook for two months. The bills didn't get paid."

Pam's office was fun and full of energy, with everyone chatting with each other all the time, but the work wasn't getting done. She also hired more people than she needed. She had someone to type articles, another to answer the phones, several to sell, a supervisor to run the office, even someone to come in and water the plants. "My expenses were ridiculous," Pam said. "Clients didn't come to me, I went to them. There was no reason to have that many people." She reduced her staff to three. Then Pam started hiring people strong in the areas in which she was weak or had no interest. "It was almost like hiring your opposite," she said. Pam was more comfortable talking than writing, so she dictated her letters, speeches, and other material into a tape recorder and had an assistant transcribe and polish the work in writing. "When hiring, I asked for people who could type," she said. "My first typist couldn't spell. A lot of people don't check that."

When Pam needed an outside accounting firm, she asked a friend she trusted for a referral. That friend recommended someone in another state, but the long-distance relationship worked well with e-mail, faxes, and telephones, Pam said. She paid a monthly retainer to the firm, which did all her bookkeeping. "A reasonably priced accountant is worth it," she said. "He saves you on taxes, and you have no problem if audited." Pam had an outside attorney she trusted, also in a different state, whom she paid an hourly rate rather than a retainer to review every contract. The advances in technology made these business relationships possible, she said.

Eventually, Pam's husband, Rick, a former geophysicist with a head for business, came aboard to handle the business side of the company, leaving Pam free to concentrate on sales, consulting, and training. But Pam never delegated the part of her business that was her strength and that she loved most—the training—even though it meant she was on the road ten days a month. "I had seen too many people get so involved in the paperwork of the business that they stopped doing something they loved and then lost the passion, the drive that made them good at what they did," she explained.

The problem with running such a lean company was the absence of "atta boys," Pam said. "You don't have someone looking over your shoulder criticizing you, but you also don't have someone patting you on the back," she said. "The entrepreneur has to be self-motivated."

66. IT'S POLICY

A business should have written policies
and procedures from the start.

■ ■ ■

After working as a claims supervisor for an insurance company, Steve Salem joined his father's temporary employment agency, Rudy Salem Staffing Services, in Sioux City, Iowa, in 1987. Rudy ran the business informally, without written policies and procedures. That approach made the company vulnerable to employees who overstepped their bounds, wanted more vacation than they had earned, or did their jobs poorly, said Steve, who bought out his father in 1991.

Many small-business owners actively resist writing policies and procedures. They hated them when they worked in big corporations, and by golly, they're not going to be hog-tied by them in their own companies. Others have been warned by attorneys that written policies will only get them into trouble. Poorly written policies certainly can cause trouble, but lack of any written policies or procedures can cause more trouble, both legal and organizational. Even the smallest employer has the legal responsibility not to discriminate and not to tolerate sexual harassment. Companies with as few as 15 employees must abide by the Americans with Disabilities Act in hiring. You don't waive your obligation if you avoid putting these rules in writing; you merely leave supervisors uninformed of their duties. The most significant benefit of rules and procedures is that they ensure everyone has the same vision and is moving in the same direction. If you, as owner, don't establish the vision and direction, your workers will make up their own. Companies flounder without procedural road maps. In an increasingly litigious society, they can sink under the weight of lawsuits for discrimination, sexual harassment, and wrongful termination. Sixty percent of U.S. employers were defendants in employment practices lawsuits in the 1990s alone. Many of those problems arose because employees misunderstand what they were told or believed they had been treated unfairly. The employee handbook, for example, should specify employee benefits. "Some people won't even take the vacations to which they're entitled," Steve said. "Others take all their vacation and want more. You end up with divisiveness between the martyrs and the abusers."

Companies need to write their policies clearly, in plain English, and enforce them uniformly. The sooner companies establish these formal procedures and policies, the better. "We found it difficult to change our informal culture despite the need to do so. It's better to start out the way you eventually hope to end up," Steve concluded.

When writing employee policies, business owners must carefully avoid any potentially discriminatory language. Also, they should make sure they can live with any policies they write and follow what they have written. For example, your firm has a policy that any employee caught stealing will be fired. Then you catch Joe with his hand in the till, but you let him off with a warning because he's a hard worker. If you catch another employee stealing and fire him, he can claim a breach of good faith and fair dealing because you treated Joe differently.

Policies should avoid any wording that restricts an owner's discretion in dealing with issues. If policies contain lists—for example, causes of termination—those lists should be labeled as examples, not all-inclusive inventories. Policies also should include consequences for violation, such as progressive discipline leading to dismissal for continued poor work performance. However, the focus must be on employee behavior on the job.

Company policy can't specify termination for a worker who drinks in his spare time if the drinking doesn't affect his job performance. If you have trouble defining your own policies and procedures, you might consider hiring consultants, as Steve did, to help put your company on a more formal track. Although the bulk of Salem Staffing's business had been in finding temporary workers for client companies, consultants helped Steve expand the company's base to permanent job placement, executive searches, and on-the-job safety consulting. The company was sold in 2003.

67. SIDE ONE: GET A PARTNER

The best partnerships are business arrangements, not friendships, to which each member brings different skills.

■ ■ ■

Roger Faubel and Meg Waters both had years of media relations experience when they found themselves working on the same major project in 1998. Waters and Faubel in Lake Forest, California, just had a fictitious business name but no formal partnership for a year. Finally, the pair did set out a formal partnership agreement. "I'd work on faith without a contract, and he wouldn't," Meg said. "We would be ruined if I ran things."

One of the greatest values of a partnership is pooled financial contributions and shared duties. When a good match comes together, the result is greater than the sum of the parts. However, many partnerships begin in friendship and end in a feud. While it is important for partners to like and trust each other, they also should be clear about their expectations and the contributions each makes to the company. One shouldn't do all the work or even the lion's share because resentment will likely follow. Often, each partner contributes a special talent, a type of experience, or contacts that are beneficial to the company. In fact, more problems are likely to arise when all partners have the same interest and skills. If everyone wants to be a marketer, who will handle the finances or employee relations? These contributions should have value in the partnership agreement just as money does because they help determine the delegation of management duties. At Waters and Faubel, Roger was great with financial details, and

Meg was great with project details. He took the lead in bringing in new clients. She handled many of the details of client care once the relationship was formed. She described it as "getting the wash out." The agency did a great deal of media relations work on political issues and election campaigns. One major land-use campaign involved voluminous environmental impact reports. Meg was one of the few who read every word.

Both Roger and Meg were lively, gregarious characters. They appreciated each other's quirks and habits, but they preferred to leave their relationship at the office. "Roger was a friend, and I loved him to pieces, but we were not social friends," Meg said. "He didn't call and say, 'Come over for a barbecue.' Distance is important. I didn't encourage the staff to be together 24/7." When Meg went through a divorce, Roger knew about it but she didn't give him daily updates. "I wouldn't do that with a woman partner either," she said. By the same token, Meg was respectful of Roger's relationship with his wife, remembering a friend who resented her husband's partner getting involved in their personal life to the point of helping plan birthday parties.

It is valuable to keep partner relationships on a professional level because business is sometimes transient, Meg said. If they decide to go in different directions, partners who were never buddies are more likely to part on friendly terms without taking the split personally. "Women tend to think that partnerships are forever, but you have to be realistic. It's not about love; it's about business. Roger and I were great partners, and we would always be friends, even if the partnership didn't last. That's why it was important to have a written agreement with all the *T*s crossed ahead of time. If you are partners with someone who wasn't your friend before, you are more conscious about protecting yourself."

68. FLIP SIDE: FORGET A PARTNER

A partnership can be a disaster if the parties
ignore the need for a written agreement.

■ ■ ■

Roy Robbins had the entrepreneurial itch. He was tired of his job as senior process engineer at a huge aerospace company and had developed a five-year plan to leave corporate America to start a bookstore. Roy had collected books for 15 years and worked part time in bookstores to learn the business. When his employer offered a voluntary buyout in 1992, he grabbed it. Roy started Badmoon Books, a mail-order and Internet bookseller specializing in collectible editions of horror stories and mysteries. Although the business was based in his Anaheim, California, home, he hosted author book signings at standard bookstores.

A friend from the aerospace company also was interested in book retailing and had the cash and expertise to team up on a regular store, so Roy jumped into the partnership. Never again, he said. "That partnership was a major mistake." Friendship isn't enough to sustain a partnership. In fact, partnerships have been known to kill lifelong friendships. After their bookstore faltered and finally closed, Roy and his ex-partner weren't enemies, but they never talked. "It's very hard to make a partnership work, anyway," Roy said, "and when people have different goals and values, they will clash."

Successful partnerships need written agreements from the beginning. Unsuccessful partnerships need them even more. A typical partnership agreement should state a specific purpose for the business, each partner's tangible (money, property, equipment, patents) and intangible (services, special skills, contacts) contributions, and each partner's percentage of the business in return for those contributions. Such agreements can be structured so one partner owns a bigger share than the others do. The agreement should also specify each partner's management responsibilities and whether he or she can have outside business activities. Roy, for example, continued his mail-order business. Perhaps most important, the agreement should specify how partners can end their arrangement. Like partners in marriage, partners in business don't like to talk about divorce ahead of time, but these decisions can be made more fairly up front, uncolored by the rancor that can build through the experience. If one partner dies or wants out, the remaining partners should have the opportunity to buy his or her share. Some successful, long-time partnerships run into trouble when one partner dies and his heirs, who have never been involved before, insist on joining the business. The agreement also should determine how a departing partner's share would be valued and paid. Often, partnerships end bitterly; some issues just cannot be resolved. A written partnership agreement can save the partners the time and expense of a lawsuit by spelling out a means for resolving disputes, usually arbitration or mediation. Even if partners are relatives or best friends, they should have separate attorneys review the agreement before signing.

Roy attributed many of their differences to a personality clash. He was much happier running Badmoon Books by himself—even if it meant starting work at 5:00 AM to respond to e-mail from his European customers or working three days straight when he had to publish a new catalog. But, then, he had no hassles if he wanted to go to one of his son's activities. "You have to be driven to be a small-business owner," Roy said.

69. TRUST BUT VERIFY

A small business must trust employees, but set up
financial checks and balances to thwart embezzlement.

■ ■ ■

Michael Barrow is fortunate to be alive. He was fortunate even to have a business after his only employee embezzled more than $109,000 from his independent insurance agency, MTB Insurance in Orange, California. Although circumstances converged that overcame Michael's normal conservative, conscientious ownership style, his experience illustrates how careful a business owner must be in hiring employees and then in setting up financial safeguards to protect the business.

Michael was running his insurance agency by himself when his mother died in Florida. He was so busy juggling clients and his mother's estate that he hired an office manager quickly and without checking her references. Within a few weeks, the new employee forged Michael's name on a check written on his mother's account and then started forging his name on checks written against the business bank account. She forged more than 160 checks in 18 months, Michael said.

Banks have fraud detection systems, but many of them process millions of checks daily, so they rely on account holders to report forgeries, stolen checks, and other suspicious activity. Generally, if the owner doesn't handle all financial work himself, he should assign a different person to reconcile the bank account than the one who pays the bills. The owner should open all bank statements personally and reconcile the account with returned checks immediately. Michael did review returned checks, but the embezzling office manager withheld the forged checks, claiming they hadn't been returned yet. Michael was so busy running his agency that he forgot about those checks by the next month's statement. The embezzler wrote checks for cash, but entered them in the company checkbook as office supplies. She used company credit cards to replenish the business checking account. She also used checks that were often enclosed with the credit card statements. She changed the address on some of the credit cards to a post office box and applied for two other cards in Michael's name using that same post office box. Michael didn't see the actual credit card statements because the office manager prepared a monthly list of company bills for him to pay. The embezzler started eating lunch at her desk and going into the office on Saturdays to intercept the mail. Once, the mail arrived and Michael started thumbing through it. The office manager cried that he was doing her job.

Michael finally discovered the embezzlement when he tried to refinance his house and discovered $58,000 on his credit cards. He filed a criminal complaint and cooperated with the office manager's prosecution. He also spent hundreds of hours unraveling the crime and dealing with creditors. He believed the stress contributed to his developing cancer of the vocal cords in the midst of the unfolding financial crisis.

After the former employee was convicted, Michael weighed whether to urge the court to send her to jail or allow house arrest. "I wanted her to go to jail, but the district attorney said if she was in jail she wouldn't be able to work and repay me," Michael said. She repaid most of the money, which was better than most embezzlement victims received. The court ordered her to tell future employers about the embezzlement and prohibited her from handling money for any business or charity.

Michael beat the cancer, rebuilt his business, and paid off all his debts. He used the services of a payroll company, even when he only had one employee. He handled the bills himself. "I think the only thing that kept me going was the support of my family and friends," he said. "The sign over my door said, 'You never fail until you stop trying.'"

70.   TAKE CARE OF THE CHILD

Home-based business owners must eliminate the crying baby, barking dog, and friendly neighbor, all of whom steal professionalism and concentration.

■ ■ ■

In 1988, Toni Korby started Antonia Korby Design, Inc., making curtains and bedspreads in her Centreville, Virginia, home, so she could be with her children, who were one and three years old at the time. A third baby was born two years later. "The whole purpose of working out of the home was to take care of my kids," Toni said, "but if I were to do it again, I would have paid more attention to childcare sooner."

Thousands of women and men start home-based businesses for lifestyle reasons such as care of small children or elderly parents. They often discover that home life and business are not completely compatible. Unless the entrepreneur deals honestly with these incompatibilities, one or the other—perhaps both—will suffer.

Toni had to strike a balance between work time and childcare time. "I tried all kinds of arrangements," she said. "I took my daughter to a woman's house. Preschool allowed my children to stay through lunch, so I got a block of four hours to work in the mornings every other day." One summer, Toni hired a woman to watch the children in her home, but "that didn't work out well," she said. "I could still hear the kids. It was very distracting."

Most clients don't care where their suppliers are based. They will take your business as seriously as you do, regardless of where it is headquartered. Clients merely ask that the work be done correctly and on time. Toni never hid that she worked from home, as home-based business owners used to do in past decades. Two factors are at work on the home-based enterprise, however. One is the appearance of professionalism. There are no barking dogs or crying babies in high-rise offices. The other is the owner's ability to work under chaotic conditions. Home often is more hectic than a corporate office.

Some huge enterprises had humble home-based beginnings. Milton Hershey started making candy in his kitchen. Steve Jobs and Stephen

Wozniak made the first Apple computer in Jobs's garage. Your enterprise could grow to be as big as theirs if you treat it seriously. Home-based business owners usually blow their credibility by failing to separate personal life and business. They don't get the licenses or fictitious business names to form their businesses legally. They don't keep regular business hours. They don't have separate business telephone lines that they answer professionally. And the notion of a home-based business solving childcare problems is a myth. Entrepreneur parents find themselves making business calls during naptime, using day care centers to grab some uninterrupted work hours, and calling on neighbors or babysitters when a business crisis arises.

In some areas, home-business owners form informal alliances or formal clubs to share childcare duties. Perhaps one parent takes the children on Monday and Wednesday mornings and the other takes them Tuesday and Thursday afternoons, freeing up uninterrupted time for appointments or production without worries of child safety. If anything, the entrepreneur parent must work faster and be more organized than other business owners. "I called it the juggle-juggle act," Toni said. "I became better at time management. I planned my schedule to drop something off at one client's place on the way to another appointment, for example."

71. LINK WITH OTHERS

Strategic alliances will help finance a start-up.

■ ■ ■

When single mother Diana Todaro didn't want her son to eat a lot of sugary, high-fat junk food, she created her own cookies from whole grains, nuts, and dried fruits. She figured that moms everywhere probably were looking for wholesome snacks made without preservatives or artificial flavors, so in 1990, she used her recipes to launch Diana's California Cookies in Laguna Hills, California. Diana's Cookies wasn't Nabisco. She financed the start-up out of her own pocket. She handled the sales and marketing herself. One of her brothers was company attorney. Another brother was financial advisor. Diana sold more than a million cookies in her first three months in business.

But without the help of unrelated companies, Diana's Cookies never would have gotten off the ground. The first alliance Diana made was with a contract bakery. This arrangement saved her company the expense of leasing, building, or buying a factory and warehouse. After trial runs in several U.S. supermarket chains, Diana started her own distribution through toll-free phone service and mail order. She also started selling her cookies under the labels of other cookie companies—more important alliances to help Diana's Cookies grow.

A one-time travel agent who had visited 25 foreign countries, Diana made international expansion a part of her company's growth plan from the start. To better understand her overseas customers, Diana returned to college to get a master's degree in international trade for small business. "Don't just read magazine articles; go back to school," she advised. "You need to be with people who want to do what you do." Diana originally tried to find a distributor in Denmark because she had lived in the country for a year. Danes were interested only in butter cookies, however, not the Fudgy Chocolate Chunk cookies, Luscious Lemon Coconut cookies, Zesty Mandarin Orange Almond cookies, Macadamia Nut Chunk cookies, or other selections in Diana's Cookies' collection.

"Large companies can [export] on their own, but small companies can get so much help from the government," Diana said, referring to an important alliance with the U.S. Department of Commerce. Diana paid $1,700 plus travel expenses to participate in a trade mission to Northern Ireland in 1995. She and executives from 15 other American companies met business representatives from all over Ireland. For Diana, that led to a well-published partnership with a Northern Ireland cookie company in 1996. She agreed to introduce that baker's crackers into the United States, and it would make and distribute her cookies throughout Europe. "I believe in long-standing relationships," Diana said. "Relationships are everything in business." Relationships you can trust are especially important in international trade, she said. The distance alone, plus language and cultural barriers, make exporting different from tracking U.S. markets. "You can't check on things overseas like you can domestically. Here, I jumped in my car and drove to the bakery," she said. "You have to rely on the partner at the other end to jump if problems arise. It's time and money. You can't fly overseas all the time." Diana learned this lesson the hard way when her Irish partner ran into financial problems a year into their agreement and eventually closed. After she spent the better part of the 1990s obtaining international trademarks for the Diana's California Cookies name and logo and developing relationships on three continents, Diana was not about to abandon the globalization of her products. Through an alliance with a Hong Kong distributor, the cookies were introduced into mainland China. She also developed strategic partnerships with other companies to sell to the United Kingdom, Europe, Mexico, and Japan. "Originally, [exporting] takes longer than domestic deals," Diana said, "but once you start, the opportunities are endless."

72. FIND YOUR PIONEERS

Establish relationships with distributors and other people who believe in your new product enough to pioneer it to others.

■ ■ ■

The buyer for the large retail chain confessed that he regularly used Ronn King's paint stirrer, called the Squirrel Mixer, at home, but he wouldn't stock it in his stores. King's firm, Site-b Company, in Spokane, Washington, was just another one-product manufacturer in an age when large retailers and distributors want to limit their number of suppliers. They would rather buy a thousand products from one supplier than two each from 500 different manufacturers.

All inventors know the frustrations associated with turning their ideas into tangible products. The fact that retailers then greet their brainchildren with indifference or hostility chases many away. Ronn spent 15-hour days for more than a year trying to break through this final barrier to market. But he couldn't do it alone. Credible salespeople had to be willing to be the first—the pioneers, as Ronn called them—to take on a product with unproven customer appeal.

It all began when Ronn, looking for a better way to stir paint, attached a metal stick on a plastic cylinder that looked like a pet rodent's exercise wheel. Slats on the cylinder stirred the paint quickly and completely when the stick was turned. Its appearance inspired the invention's name: the Squirrel Mixer. Initially, Ronn tried to sell directly to buyers for major home-improvement retailers. One after another turned him down. To prove that customers would buy the Squirrel Mixer, Ronn started selling it by mail order and persuaded some independent paint stores to carry it. Soon salespeople for distribution companies saw the Squirrel Mixer in several stores and started asking about it. Even then, however, their bosses didn't call Ronn; he had to call them.

One breakthrough came from a buyer who rejected the Squirrel Mixer, but referred Ronn to a manufacturer's representative that carried dozens of products for many companies. The representative not only liked the Squirrel Mixer enough to carry it in his line, he gave Ronn the names of sales representatives in other geographic areas. These pioneering independent representatives helped Ronn get the product into stores and attract distributors. That distribution relationship is important to any manufacturer because while independent representatives take orders for a product, distributors actually buy it and stock it in their warehouses—a real cash-flow plus. But distributors must make money too. Generally, they look for products that are similar to other products in their lines or that will sell in huge volume. Minus such an attraction, however, a distributor might accept a product that has a high profit margin and falls in a lucrative niche market the distributor wants to expand. The manufacturer also might have to offer incentives, such as one free case of product for every ten ordered or money for co-op advertising. Even after distributors and retailers add on their profit margins, though, the product still must sell for a price consumers will pay.

Ronn, with the help of his pioneers, sold 60,000 mixers in the first year and moved into The Home Depot chain. He also signed agreements with major paint companies, such as Red Devil, to put their labels on his product, which opened their distribution channels to the Squirrel Mixer and moved it into even more stores. Even with a proven product, selling to major retailers was a continuing problem, Ronn said. Many retailers and distributors sat on the sidelines waiting for the small manufacturer to sell product rights to a big company or sign private-label agreements like Site-b's with Red Devil. Ronn had the good fortune to have people ask for different types and sizes of the Squirrel Mixer for uses he never imagined. Some factories wanted to attach a steel mixer to large motors to stir thousand-gallon drums of coatings and other materials. Food makers wanted Squirrel Mixers for commercial baking. But those industries had completely different sales representatives and distributors, so Ronn had to build relationships all over again.

73. BUILD WITH BOARDS

A board of outside advisors can help an entrepreneur
grow the business faster and smarter.

■ ■ ■

Leroy Knuths was a partner at one of the nation's largest accounting firms, but what he really wanted to do was run his own company—a manufacturing company, not another accounting practice. In 1980, he and some partners bought Rosco Manufacturing, which made road maintenance equipment, and moved it to Madison, South Dakota. "I wanted to form an outside board of advisors from the beginning, but my partners weren't interested," Leroy said. "I finally had to buy them out in order to set up an outside board."

Major corporations have boards of directors, but few entrepreneurs realize the value of an informal board of advisors even in a small company. This group doesn't dictate, it counsels and collaborates. If put together properly, the advisors bring experience, knowledge, and objectivity that the business owner lacks. "I was very selective with whom I asked to be on my board," Leroy said. Rosco Manufacturing's board of advisors had three members. One was the former president of a Rosco competitor. Leroy knew this advisor's abilities well, and the advisor knew Rosco well. The second advisor was a business owner with strong sales and marketing skills. Originally, the third advisor was a technical expert in manufacturing for the road construction industry. When he retired in 1997, the advisor recommended another technical expert. Some business owners have more advisors, depending on their needs; however, large groups can be unwieldy. Besides, "It's not easy to recruit people of this caliber," Leroy said. "Part of the attraction for them is your own credibility and reputation."

Rosco's advisors met quarterly, and Leroy paid them $1,000 apiece. Other entrepreneurs whose companies are young or financially strapped pay less or just buy lunch for their advisors. Such experts usually aren't in it for the money. Some companies issue stock to their advisors. Leroy didn't take that route because he didn't want his advisors to have a financial interest in the advice they gave. Also, stock ownership raises liability issues that many advisors want to avoid.

To make best use of a board of advisors, a business owner must be strong enough that the board doesn't dominate or pursue personal agendas. However, the owners also must want and use the help offered. Many business owners are secretive about their company operations; however, if they want their advisory boards to be useful, they must be candid, willing to share information, and open to change. "You must be genuinely interested," Leroy said. "They only come on board on the condition that you listen to them."

With his board's help, Leroy doubled the company, and expanded overseas, including to Russia, which suffered economically, in part, because its road infrastructure was so poor that products couldn't be moved easily from plant to market. Rosco Manufacturing made asphalt distributors, sweepers, rollers, and other large equipment to build and repair the country's roads.

"My board of advisors injected a whole lot of great ideas on the marketing side and the manufacturing side," Leroy said. "I knew we needed more sales emphasis, and they certainly supported that. They helped me hire a new sales manager." The most difficult part about working with outside advisors is setting aside personal ego and sensitivities. "You have to have broad shoulders and thick skin," Leroy said, "and be willing to bite your tongue at times."

Leroy died in 2001, the company was sold and moved in 2003 to North Carolina.

PART 6

MARKETING

■ ■ ■

Money is the most obvious need of a new business, but marketing is the most overlooked. In fact, marketing may be more essential than money. No one will give you money until they know you exist, and no one will know your company exists until you announce it. That's marketing. Just as significant, without marketing, no one will know that your products and services satisfy his or her greatest desires and overcome his or her greatest fears.

Marketing begins with market research—knowing who wants what you're selling. It continues with targeting—figuring out who's most likely to buy. It moves on to planning—determining how your likely customer makes buying decisions.

The well-crafted marketing plan combines the benefits of your products and services with the right combination of message delivery channels. Today's consumer is so bombarded with information that you need to choose carefully what you say and how, when, and where you say it.

I can feel you tensing up already. Relax. Many business owners discover that marketing becomes the greatest fun of their work lives.

74.

THE MYTH OF
THE BETTER MOUSETRAP

Just because you build a better product than competitors
doesn't mean the world will beat a path to your door.

■ ■ ■

Engineer David Giuliani was skeptical when University of Washington professors David Engel and Roy Martin asked him to head a company to develop their new electric toothbrush. The home electric toothbrush market was large, but so was the competition. Braun, Teledyne, and Bausch & Lomb all had viable entries backed by far more money than this trio had. Yeah, but Engel and Martin's idea was to blast bacteria with sound waves, not scrub it off. Unfortunately, their technology didn't work. David Giuliani continued his day job at Abbott Labs and spent his free time turning that idea into a viable product for his new company, Optiva Corporation in Bellevue, Washington. He spent two years developing a workable technology for the Sonicare Toothbrush—and that was the easy part.

Most consumers don't go looking for new products, especially $130 toothbrushes. They must be wooed to a new product or way of doing things with strong, continuous, well-conceived marketing. "It's hard to get a new product to market," David said. "We had more roadblocks than many, but, on average, it was what one should expect in developing a new product." Optiva lacked the huge marketing budgets of its larger competitors, so it decided to market to dentists by advertising in dental journals and hiring a few salespeople to call on the dentists. The company didn't have a great deal of quantitative data, but cofounder David Engel was a periodontist with a good industry reputation. Dentists who tried Sonicare swore by it. "Marketing has to be done in sequence and at a certain rate," David Giuliani said. "If we moved too fast, we would have irritated dentists."

While dentists would push the market, Optiva wanted to create some consumer interest to pull it. "Many dentists took Sonicare seriously because they had a patient whose gums looked great, and when they asked, 'What are you doing, flossing?' the patients said, 'I bought a Sonicare.'" Optiva began creating this consumer interest by mailing ads in millions of credit card billing statements. The result was only 11 sales. Obviously,

Sonicare's benefits couldn't be pitched in a brief ad; therefore, in 1995, the company turned to infomercials—30-minute program-like commercials that heavily stressed research results, which the company had by this time, and expert recommendations. "We had a few testimonials, but the average viewer would just think we paid someone to say good things, so the experts and research were more important," David said. A year earlier, Optiva sponsored Paul Harvey's radio show. Harvey often did his own commercials, and his audience was older when dental disease is a common problem, David said. "We didn't have a reputation, so we needed a spokesperson with a preexisting reputation, like Paul Harvey had."

By 1996, Sonicare held 33 percent of the U.S. electric toothbrush market, second only to Braun. David grew the company to $175 million in sales and 600 employees and helped create another thousand jobs at surrounding small and mid-sized companies. In 2000, Dutch consumer products giant Philips Electronics bought Optiva to add Sonicare to its stable of oral care products.

75. MARKETING NEEDS A PLAN TOO

Even if your venture has a business plan, it needs a strong marketing plan too.

■ ■ ■

Kathy Donoghue traveled a great deal as operations manager for a major computer company. During one trip, she read in an in-flight magazine about the National Association of Professional Organizers and thought she should start that type of consulting practice. In 1988, she and partner Judy Nevins opened Another Alternative in Alden, New York, to train, consult, and teach seminars on time management and the organizing process.

Although the partners wrote a business plan, which included a section on marketing, the company would have attracted more business if they had written a much stronger, separate marketing plan, Kathy said. "We all think we have the best thing to offer and everyone will realize it," she said.

"But especially with a new service business, we had to sell ourselves and our services almost from scratch."

The marketing portion of most business plans plays a minor supporting role to issues of management, financing, and product or service. However, some experts argue that you can't really write a business plan until you have identified someone to buy what you want to sell. In fact, you should write a separate marketing plan each time you introduce a new product or service or enter a new geographic or demographic market. The plan doesn't have to be long or formal, but it should establish your strategy so you effectively reach the people most likely to buy from you.

Marketing has five elements: product (what you're selling), package, promotion (how you reach potential buyers), price, and place (where you'll sell the product and how you'll get it there). Different companies place different emphasis on these elements in their marketing. The well-prepared marketing plan specifies what is unique about your product or service. It identifies the size of your expected market, by segment, and the share you can reasonably expect to capture. It lists major competitors, why customers buy from them, and their sales, growth rates, and market shares. The plan describes your most likely customers, why they will buy from you, and which forms of promotion and advertising will most effectively reach them. But no marketing plan is complete without a timetable, budget, and means for measuring results. Without a strong marketing plan, Another Alternative lacked an efficient, effective strategy for growing with limited funds. "When we first started, people didn't know what we did. We had to work hard to establish the need in people's minds," Kathy said. "A strong marketing plan would have classified the most productive ways to educate potential clients to their need for organizational help. When I went in [to a client's business] I wore different hats going through the [consulting] process. I started as analyst, then teacher and coach, then reviewer to make sure they kept on track."

Kathy originally focused her attention on individuals rather than companies. "If people don't change, nothing changes," she explained. However, trying to train one person at a time wasn't very lucrative and achieves limited results. To grow Another Alternative and accomplish bigger results for her clients, Kathy needed to help an entire department or company organize its strategies. A marketing plan could have helped her identify that market sooner. As it was, Kathy started with small companies, and then worked up to bigger projects and clients. "The more work I did, the more people referred me," she said. "I taught a lot of seminars and workshops, which brought more business, but I couldn't become a presenter until I had the experience." Kathy's strategy to obtain referrals could have been part of her marketing plan, too.

76.

MARKETING IS
AN INVESTMENT

Don't choose your marketing efforts based on how
much they cost. Calculate the return on investment.

■   ■   ■

While working as an interviewer and job counselor in the early 1970s, Patty DeDominic loved listening to people's dreams and matching them to the right job. In a later job as a corporate trainer, she loved the interaction with businesspeople. Later still she advised employment services. That's when Patty realized that instead of doing this work for other companies, she should do it for her own. In 1979, she opened PDQ Personnel Services as a temporary-employment agency in Los Angeles, California. "I began consulting with staffing services, then I thought I should do it for myself," Patty said. "I would have gained more business sooner if I had invested money in marketing and business development from the start."

Few new business owners who don't have marketing backgrounds think of business marketing as an investment. They look at a marketing plan's price tag, emit a low whistle, and say, "Wow! That's expensive." The truth is they don't know whether it's expensive; they know what they expect to spend. In most cases, they don't have as much start-up capital as they need, but they don't know how much that marketing expenditure is worth to the company in terms of revenue, prestige, contacts, and visibility.

If you put $100 in a government-insured savings account at 3 percent interest, you know you'll have $103 at the end of the term. If you invest it in a gas exploration firm, you might triple your money or lose it all. You are weighing risk versus potential gain. You can do the same when you look at marketing as an investment. You don't merely throw money into telephone directory ads, billboards, and direct mail pieces; you assess the likelihood of getting business from those efforts. How much business? What kind of business? Will you get more business from a quarter-page ad in a newspaper or a trade journal? Once you have run the ad or sent the direct mail piece, you can evaluate the results in terms of value to your company to determine how you'll spend your marketing dollars next time. Marketing becomes an ever increasingly precise investment instead of money tossed into a black hole.

Patty and her staff started holding annual marketing strategy meetings. They weighed whether and how much money and effort PDQ Services should put into public relations, advertisements, and sales. Then they put their decisions in writing. "We wanted to make sure that our strategy for the year was the backbone of all our marketing to reinforce and leverage our message," Patty said. She chose different media to get the message across. "One year, we made a major commitment to radio advertising. The next, to billboards, direct mail, and telemarketing." Patty carefully monitored the business growth that could be attributed to each of her advertising efforts. This evaluation required every marketing application to include some measurement means. That's why radio ads sometimes end with "mention this ad and get a 10 percent discount." That's why direct mail pieces often contain discount coupons. That's why some magazine ads list mailbox numbers for orders. The same ad in different publications has different mailbox numbers.

Sales may not be the only way you measure the worth of your marketing endeavors. Patty served on the boards for local, state, and women's business organizations, which gave PDQ Services broad visibility. However, that time investment had value beyond the business bottom line. "When there was an alignment between my personal beliefs and the organization's business purposes, I was much more likely to be involved and encourage my staff to be involved," Patty said.

77.

THE WORLD IS
NOT YOUR MARKET

There's not enough money or time in the world for companies
to market themselves successfully as all things to all people.

■ ■ ■

As a college student in the 1970s, Martha Daniel wanted to run the
information services department of a major corporation someday. However, after working her way up several corporate ladders, she thought she
could do better as boss of the whole business. So in 1992, Martha launched
Information Management Resources, Inc., to provide computer-consulting
services to large corporations, including some of her old employers.
"When you're a new company, you're building your business off relationships. Whatever they want, you do," Martha said. "But I was absolutely too
scattered."

Martha was like many new business owners—unwilling to focus on a
niche for fear of missing a sale. So they waste time and money trying to
sell everything to everyone. The result is often bankruptcy, burnout, or
both. "I needed a niche, so I looked back at the work we had done and saw
the types of jobs we had done most," Martha said. She defined several related services for the core business of Information Management Resources, based in Costa Mesa, California, with offices in four other states
and Washington D.C. The company would concentrate on systems integration, training, and financial and custom software.

One of the company's original services that Martha let go was telecommunications because it didn't fit with her company's strengths or clients' demands. Martha chose to hang on to related services, however,
which enabled Information Management Resources to gain additional
work with existing clients. Past buyers are the most likely future buyers, so
marketing to them costs a fraction of the expense of corralling new customers. If Information Management Resources developed a piece of custom software, Martha explained, the client needed to have it integrated into
the company's existing hardware and software system and to have employees trained to use it. Information Management Resources had the inside
track of winning that additional work. Such targeting shortens a company's

sales cycle and devotes time and personal attention to the people most likely to buy a product or service. "Narrowing my service offerings [in the beginning] would have enabled me to present a manageable marketing plan," Martha said. "Additionally, my clients would have viewed the business differently—as a specialist, not a generalist."

Specialists can command higher pay rates and greater attention than generalists. They also tend to have less competition. You can develop a better understanding of your target market by asking yourself the five Ws: Who is your customer? What does this customer need and want? Where will the customer expect to find you? When is the customer likely to have this need? Why will the customer choose you? Timing, too, can influence a company's marketing focus. In the late 1990s, Martha emphasized her company's ability to resolve the Year 2000 problem for older computer systems. For a while that division represented 35 percent of her company's work. But after the turn of the millennium the company dropped that obsolete specialty. That adjustment illustrates a good point about marketing. You're not stuck forever doing the same old things you've always done. You must periodically reevaluate your niche and adjust because customer needs and markets change.

78. RELATIONSHIP MARKETING

While developing relationships is a good marketing
strategy, it requires more research, planning,
and effort than new business owners anticipate.

■　■　■

After two decades working in marketing and training jobs for international corporations, Jeff Zakaryan spent two years carefully planning to start his own company. While the corporate experience was valuable, Jeff learned the real meaning of total responsibility after establishing Global Strategies, an executive performance consulting firm in Dana Point, California, in 1997.

He had little success in marketing his services through direct mail advertising or general networking meetings. He discovered that most of his business came from building relationships not just with clients but also with those around them.

Relationship marketing is applying the Golden Rule—treat others as you want to be treated—on a consistent basis. Some entrepreneurs report that relationship marketing gives as much as a 50 percent return on investment. Better still, they have a circle of lifelong friends. The person who has the power to make the decision to hire a consultant is the bull's eye, Jeff explained, but he or she is surrounded by concentric circles of influence: subordinate executives, receptionists, even parking attendants.

"I spent a lot of time with the personal touch," Jeff said. "There was a breadth and depth to the way I approached relationships with clients and the people I met." When he met with a person, he sat down that night and wrote a thank you note. Instead of Christmas cards, he sent birthday cards. He and his wife, Barbara, invited clients and their spouses to the Zakaryan home for dinner. When Jeff stopped to analyze where his business was coming from, he discovered the value of this relationship building. "These people were opening doors for me that they didn't open for others," Jeff said. "They were unsolicited advocates for me. They were giving me priority access." The nature of Jeff's consulting work brought him into contact with more than the chief executive within a company. He met and built relationships with employees other than his direct client, which was helpful if that client moved to another company. Jeff still had champions within the original company.

The wise entrepreneur maintains friendly relationships with former clients, acquaintances, and even employees because their need for products or services changes over time. But assuming you do quality work, the person most likely to hire you is someone you have worked with in the past. In some cases, a client might call after three or five years. You can encourage these calls by being proactive in keeping in touch. You can call or write not always to beg for work but to share a piece of information you know the client will find interesting or to follow up on some personal experience you know they were going through.

"This strategy really takes commitment," Jeff emphasized. "First, you'd better do good work. None of this other stuff matters if you don't do that." Second, relationship marketing must be sincere, he added. "It doesn't work if it isn't real. You have to be consistent and mean it. These people cannot become superfluous once you win the contract."

79. THE RIGHT NETWORK

Networking opportunities abound. It is important
to identify several of the most beneficial and devote
sufficient time and effort to developing them.

■ ■ ■

R. Dean Roberts decided to launch his own consulting practice, Roberts Management Solutions LLC in Hilton Head Island, South Carolina, after working 21 years for business quality expert Armand Feigenbaum. Initially, Dean used a variety of direct marketing techniques to build his clientele. He soon discovered that consulting services required the personal approach through networking. Yet that method isn't as limited as it may sound. "There are a wide variety of networking opportunities through channels that are not independent of each other or of other marketing and sales activities," Dean said. "Spend a significant amount of time identifying and evaluating a broad range of networking possibilities and actively pursue several that are aligned with your objectives."

Dean provided a range of assistance from operations to product introduction to customer relationship management. But his special expertise was quality management solutions to help companies of all sizes improve their results. He had a special love for small businesses that lacked in-house expertise.

His first networking began with family, friends, and acquaintances. "This networking channel has the advantage of not requiring a lot of research and can quickly identify specific prospects," Dean said. "Some are potential customers and many can provide references to potential customers." For example, Dean contacted the owner of a small contract manufacturer he had worked for more than two decades earlier. The owner's son provided numerous contacts. Dean also cultivated early on professional and business organizations, including his local chamber of commerce and the local chapter of the American Society for Quality. Many of the relationships he developed in both groups provided referrals and contacts. A few became clients. "In the chamber of commerce I got on the small business council, which was useful because I wanted to work with small businesses," Dean said.

His third networking channel was service and social organizations. He was active in the Rotary Club and his church. "Ethically it is not appropriate to use these groups overtly as a marketing and sales channel," he said, "so its primary value is in adding friends and acquaintances" who provide referrals. Such networking requires participation. People are more likely to do business with you if they see you in action informally in groups in which they, too, are active. That's why it is better to select a few targeted groups than to hop around to many. Some networkers concentrate on groups to which their most likely clients belong. Others prefer industry organizations. In addition, new business owners can find many opportunities to establish formal and informal affiliations either with people in the same industry or in complementary businesses, Dean said. "This type of relationship can result in mutually beneficial referencing agreements, work sharing, information sharing, (joint) advertising, and complementary businesses can be potential customers or suppliers."

The fledgling business owner should also explore organizations that offer accreditation or directory listings, Dean suggested. He received accreditation from the Institute for Independent Business. "While this may seem to stretch the definition of networks, many of them are effectively consulting resources," he said. "However, most require a financial investment. Therefore research them thoroughly to determine if they are in sync with your business and that they can produce results." Networking requires continual evaluation to make sure that your time is well spent and that the commitment is actually bringing in business. If not, you may be having fun, but it's not marketing. "You have to be aggressive in networking," Dean said. "You can't just sit back and expect business to come to you."

80. TALK TO YOUR CUSTOMERS

Survey your market before you decide
what products or services to offer.

■ ■ ■

Dave Markham, a former respiratory therapist, became so good at leading outdoor recreation trips that, in 1982, he and his wife, Sue Barney, decided to start their own travel adventure company—Venture Outdoors, in Hailey, Idaho. Dave kept his winter job at Boise State University until 1988, but each summer, he and Sue took tourists on kayaking, hiking, and bike tours. "I had a good idea what I wanted to do, but that's where I goofed," Dave said. "I picked out activities that I was most qualified to do and most enjoyed doing. I finally realized that if I was going to survive, I had to be more realistic and find out what the public wanted to do. Then I could narrow it down to what I wanted to do that people were willing to pay for."

Many new business owners plunge into their enterprises without really asking whether anyone is willing to pay for the proposed products or services. Surveys of the marketplace can save those business owners willing to heed the results a lot of money and frustration. "I couldn't afford an expensive survey, but I did read travel industry magazines to find out what the trends were," Dave said. "Unfortunately, I read what I wanted to read and ignored a lot of useful information at first."

For example, Dave learned that kayaking was growing in popularity, and because he had been kayaking since 1968, a kayak trip seemed to be a good offering. However, Dave got few registrations for his trips of intermediate skill to Alaska. Listening to prospective customers convinced him to change the activity to a trip for beginners, which was quite successful. In fact, Dave reevaluated all the vacations he offered for rugged adventurers. "We became a cushy wilderness experience," Dave said. Tour guests were treated to trail meals of raspberry French toast, orange beef, and chocolate cream pie, for example.

Although Dave didn't have a big budget for formal market surveys, he started asking anyone who called Venture Outdoors' toll-free telephone number what he or she wanted in an adventure vacation. He sent out surveys to everyone on the company's mailing list, compiled from inquiries and past tour guests. Every brochure included a short survey that the recipient could fill out and send back. "You can't ask too many questions, [though,] or people won't respond," Dave said. But every little bit of information helps, and when diligently logged and categorized, it adds up to sizeable market research.

"When we finally got people on a trip, we gave them more than we promised and then hoped they would provide us with feedback at the end of the trip, good and bad," Dave said.

Adventure travel is the fastest growing segment of the vacation industry, and many people want to take these trips with family. However, different members of each family have different levels of skill and desire for challenge, Dave said. "Maybe Dad and son want more aggressive biking side trips than Mom and daughter want," he said. "We modified every trip to accommodate those types of requests." You never know enough to stop surveying current and potential customers, Dave said. Because Idaho weather pretty much confined Venture Outdoors to summer trips in the state, Dave and Sue added winter trips to Baja, Mexico, because people requested them. "And to grow the company, we couldn't continue just as a summer program," Dave said. "We had to go outside Idaho."

81. THE RIGHT BALANCE OF TIME WELL SPENT

Entrepreneurs with technical skills have to work
hard on their marketing and presentation skills.

■ ■ ■

James Woo was a university researcher when he realized how wide the gap was between the basic research that went on in university labs and the ability to find some practical use for that research in the real world. So, in 1981, Jim formed InterScience, Inc., in Troy, New York, to bridge the gap. InterScience employees did high-tech research and development under contract with the government and private companies. They developed such projects as fiber optic medical instruments and night vision goggles. "Most of the competition for our work came from university Ph.D.s and engineers," Jim said. "We just decided to do it commercially instead of at a university, where the primary objective is teaching students, not commercializing ideas."

It was both InterScience's boon and bane that its researchers behaved like, well, researchers. "We would get turned on by exciting ideas, and we'd go off doing our thing, forgetting that if we were going to make money, somebody better want to buy it," Jim said. Scientists and engineers aren't the only people who bury themselves in the technical side of their ventures and never get out and sell themselves, their ideas, or their services. Many inventors never get their ideas to market because they leave to others the nitty gritty work of turning the ideas into reality. Anyone who starts a business because he or she is good at some skill—from a plumber to a crafts manufacturer—is vulnerable to this temptation. "It's a misconception that if you have outstanding ideas you will get contracts, especially if you're small," Jim said. "The people with projects had to know us before they brought the projects to us, and if we had a good idea, we had to know where to sell it to get R&D funding." Both required relationship building, so Jim, as president, finally had to relinquish time in the lab to beat InterScience's drums. He started spending more than half his time marketing for the company.

Entrepreneurs like Jim spend much of their time talking informally with people at business parties or industry meetings and formally during sales presentations. Jim needed to listen to what research and development projects his potential clients wanted and to tell InterScience's story well enough to win the contracts to do those projects. Entrepreneurs should speak for themselves because no one has the fire and enthusiasm that they do.

However, technically skilled business owners often must overcome one obstacle: shyness. The difference between them and glib marketeers is practice, whether alone or with a speech or drama coach. The goal is to hone a concise, compelling story about a company and its work that emphasizes the benefits to the buyer, not all the Bunsen burners and computers in the lab. These gab sessions can be scary. The reassuring fact is that both your tale and your storytelling skills improve with practice. Don't be embarrassed to rehearse your story, run through trial question and answer sessions, videotape yourself, analyze your efforts with your speech coach, and then videotape again. Over time, your delivery becomes animated. Awkward gestures become comfortable. You develop open body language, including making eye contact as you speak and not crossing your arms across your chest. However, if you're the quiet type, don't try to transform yourself into the class clown. "I learned slowly to put greater emphasis on market demands for the technology we were developing," Jim said. "The market needed to drive our research instead of the other way around."

82. HOMEMADE MARKETING

Lack of money is no excuse not to market your business.
Legwork and time must substitute for money.

■ ■ ■

Pearl White was an executive secretary for a large homebuilder when the company was sold. "The company and industry were changing. I had dreamed of owning a business for a long time; this seemed like the right time to make that dream come true," she said. On January 1, 1979, Pearl opened the doors of Confidante Keys, an Irvine, California, secretarial and administrative services firm. Pearl started with $1,000 in vacation pay from her previous employer. She was on such a tight budget that she didn't have money for advertising. Without it, though, she knew Confidante Keys was headed for an early burial. Therefore, Pearl's time and effort had to make up for the money she lacked.

Pearl's office was located in an industrial park, so she began by typing up her own simple flier describing her services, qualifications, and location, then hand delivered them to every business in the park. That brought a handful of clients. Next, she joined the local chamber of commerce. That brought a few more projects. She also agreed to be the paid coordinator for a leads group, which was a stable source of income for many years and showcased her abilities for member businesses. "Every little bit helped," Pearl said.

All marketing benefits a new business to some degree, but nothing in marketing works all the time. Many different, even small, efforts executed in a coordinated and consistent way build business. In fact, small-business owners often find that when they stop marketing, their business slows down within two months. As Pearl discovered, a financially strapped entrepreneur can still find many inexpensive ways to promote business. For example, Pearl suggested asking your existing reservoir of friends for the names of potential customers, then following up on those names. The average customer needs seven contacts before buying, so continually contact the same people in fresh ways rather than calling or mailing to a person just once before moving on. Pearl handed out business cards and calendars with her company name imprinted on them. You also can distribute discount coupons, informative articles, or useful checklists. Your contacts with customers are limited by your creativity, not your pocketbook.

Once you have a few customers, find out more about them so you can offer additional services or products that meet their needs and interests, Pearl said. Call potential customers to let them know about your sales or when you add a new service or product line for which they have expressed interest. Pearl eventually gained most of her business through referrals from existing and former clients. You can encourage people to give you more referrals by asking who they know who might want or need your products or services. Ask satisfied clients for referrals, too. Don't sit back and expect busy people to refer to you without prompting.

Pearl found that her type of business needed to be listed in the telephone directory, but those advertisements could be expensive. However, even a lower-cost, bold-lettered listing worked better than nothing, she said. Over the years, Pearl also discovered that she got better results and saved money by listing in fewer directories within her geographic area than spreading her dollars over every telephone directory in the entire region. "It was an education and expanded my understanding of my capabilities," she said. "I was able to help a lot more people than if I were in one company."

83. CUSTOMERS BY MAIL

Direct mail advertising can save a lot of marketing
money by targeting the right customers.

■ ■ ■

Talk about a mismatch: Dick Seaholm majored in art in college, but worked for 40 years in the air-conditioning industry. He hated his job; however, he had a family to raise and felt he couldn't take any chances. Finally, though, Dick made a career change, trying his hand at sales until new ownership bankrupted his employer. He then taught goal-setting seminars until attendance dried up during the recession of the early 1990s.

For a while, Dick helped out his son-in-law, who was a police officer doing screen printing on the side. Then Dick learned that the local quick-print shop was getting rid of its department that applied heat transfers to T-shirts, mugs, and signs. So, in 1995, Dick sold some real estate holdings and borrowed from a family trust to open Rich Mar Shirts & Signs, a custom heat-transfer print service, in his home in Costa Mesa, California. He and his wife, Lynn, built a modest business through networking, ads in telephone directories, and word of mouth. But direct mail advertising could have identified and reached Rich Mar's best prospects more quickly and completely for faster growth, Dick said. "The biggest obstacle we had to overcome was recognition," he said. "Our motto was 'our minimum order is one,' but people who needed small orders didn't know we existed."

Direct mail, done improperly, is junk mail. Done correctly, it is like using an advertising rifle instead of a shotgun. Before embarking on his first direct mail campaign in 1998, Dick spent a great deal of time identifying what and to whom he wanted to sell. He decided to emphasize his ability to make vinyl banners and signs. His targets were construction companies, property managers, insurance companies, and restaurants, which he identified by their industry classification codes, company size, and geographic locations.

If you're targeting companies, mail order pros recommend addressing the piece to a position instead of a name because people change jobs too often for commercial mailing lists to keep up. A U.S. Postal Service study found that people open their mail according to the return address. Direct mail must have a return address, but it doesn't have to be in the envelope's upper left-hand corner. So many direct mail professionals print the required information on the inside. The pros often send direct mail individually addressed with first-class stamps instead of printed bulk mail. Personalized addresses and first-class postage are more expensive, but the envelope is opened more often.

Rich Mar Transfers used direct mail to help level out the business's ups and downs. The company was swamped in the first quarter of the year putting players' names on uniforms for youth sports leagues. But, without marketing, business slowed in April. That was when Dick sent out his direct mail. A single mailing would be a waste of money. Dick mailed at least four times to the same list, which greatly increased response. He also mailed just 2,000 pieces at a time to avoid attracting more work than he could handle. A company that stressed how it turned orders around quickly could hardly afford to make first-time customers wait even a few weeks. "I've seen other companies that got to doing too much and were overwhelmed," Dick said. "Once you have a customer base, that's your first loyalty."

84. SIGN OF YOUR TIMES

Without a sign, a new business is invisible
even on a busy street.

■ ■ ■

After more than two decades of selling vegetable seeds in western New York state, Harold Ford was laid off. He investigated several options and had decided to buy a packing and shipping franchise when he saw a for-sale ad for a newly built independent shop. So in 1996, at the age of 59, Harold opened Postal Copy Center in a strip mall in Meridian, Idaho. At the time, Harold didn't even think about the importance of having a sign visible from the busy thoroughfare on which the shopping center sat. Neither did his fellow small-business tenants or the landlord. "Signage is so important," Harold said. "How can people find your business if you don't have a sign? I don't know how I overlooked it."

Despite other types of marketing, which included mailing coupons for free keys to new homeowners in the area, Postal Copy Center struggled to get established because of its invisibility on a busy street. Harold did put a sign on his shop, but traffic moved too fast to see it.

"We paid rent based on being on this busy street, but we didn't get any benefit from it," he said. When Harold and another merchant put out a temporary banner that violated the city's sign ordinance, Harold had to remove the banner and pay a $350 fine. "Investigate your city's sign ordinance before you go into business," Harold recommended. "Most of them are cracking down on signs, eliminating pole signs altogether, limiting their size."

Although it was not a problem for Postal Copy Center, some landlords also have sign restrictions in their leases. Because Harold's landlord was too busy to obtain the permits or order the sign, Harold and five other small tenants spent more than a year getting the city to approve and issue permits for a stucco monument sign, which sat on the ground. Postal Copy Center's portion on that sign was one foot by two feet for the cost of $400. "But anything helped," Harold said.

Actually, a sign's limited size can be a benefit. Sign experts say that few words are best because the average person looks at a sign for less than a second; the size of the letters is more important. Two-inch-high letters can be read at 50 feet, but if city ordinances allow it, letters should be three feet high to be read at a thousand feet. Colors and letter style affect a sign's readability, too. Red and yellow are the most visible colors, and short, thick letters are easier to read than thin letters close together. Postal Copy Center's letters were red and black on Lucite, which was lighted from inside for greater visibility. It was fortunate that Harold didn't insist that the sign convey every Postal Copy Center service—from packaging to tax preparation and notary public services—and product, including office supplies and cards. He just wanted a sign to alert drivers to the center's existence. Once customers found him, Harold was able to increase steadily the amount each spent in his center because of its wide variety of services and products.

85.   SPEAK UP

Public speaking and seminars help establish credibility
and visibility for owners of service businesses.

■ ■ ■

As a high school and college track athlete, Steve Yarn knew what it meant to perform in front of crowds at a high level. Perhaps that was why he was so comfortable speaking to groups of potential clients as a low-pressure, yet effective way to market his financial consulting services. Steve worked at major banks for many years, but decided he wanted to be the top decision maker in his work and life. So he formed Yarn & Company Financial in Owings Mills, Maryland. He brought to his business a lesson he learned while still a banker. Offering free seminars was an easier way to reach prospective clients than trying to get separate appointments with 30 different individuals. "My concept was to present myself as an expert, not to sell a product. These were nonselling seminars," Steve said. "This way, I was the one they wanted to talk with further about their financial plans."

Some people make a living giving speeches and seminars. But many more owners of small service companies like Steve find that these public presentations are important marketing tools for building profit centers. If these speeches and seminars are well done, they establish the owner as an expert and reach targeted audiences of potential clients. It is important to have the company name and contact information on handouts that not only enhance the presentation but participants are likely to keep.

Steve created lively, entertaining seminars on debt elimination, wealth creation, and retirement planning. He often provided a free lunch prior to his 90-minute educational seminar. He spoke to groups as large as 150 and as small as five. "I had a group of five women. I rented a stretch limo, took them to lunch at a restaurant, and they loved it," Steve said.

He found that a group of 15 to 25 people was ideal. It was still a productive use of his time and small enough that participants felt they were getting special attention. After the seminar he didn't answer too many questions that would give away what he sold in his practice. Typically, 80 percent of the people attending the seminar set up appointments to talk with him individually. Steve discovered that some people needed to meet with him three or four times before they were comfortable trusting him with their investments.

"When I started doing seminars back in the '80s, other brokers thought I was nuts," Steve said. "Later I was surprised how many financial planners used this approach."

It is important that speaking engagements and seminars reach people who need the information and services you have to offer, especially if your goal is to attract paying clients.

Steve gave seminars every two weeks. He discovered that he could reach the right audiences through churches, professional organizations, and investment clubs in Maryland and Washington, D.C. His wife, Karen, who worked with him at Yarn & Co., handled many of the speaking arrangements and scheduling.

86. THE WRITE WAY

Writing articles for targeted publications can be more
effective marketing than paid advertising.

■ ■ ■

Robert Joyce had been a business consultant and management trainer for years when a major corporation offered him a job that Robert figured would carry him until retirement. The recession of the early 1990s killed that plan when Robert was laid off. Instead of going back to his old consulting routine, however, Robert wanted a new challenge. He was intrigued by the idea of helping older people write and publish their personal and family histories as keepsakes for their children; therefore, in 1993, he established Hawthorne House in his Santa Ana, California, home to do just that. "I knew how to run a business, but I had no idea how to reach my customers," Robert said. "It was just gut instinct that people would be interested in this service."

Robert took $10,000 from his 401(k) plan to develop name identity for his company. He bought display advertising in five different magazines targeted at older Americans. Small two-inch-by-two-inch ads cost

$200 a month, so it didn't take long to spend the $10,000. "Although I got a couple of jobs, it wasn't cost effective," Robert said. "An even bigger mistake was not discontinuing the ads earlier than I did. Any money I made I poured back into more ads."

Finally, Robert discovered that the writing skill he used to create his product was also a valuable marketing device. First, he wrote a sample family history, which he showed to prospective customers. Then he found another way to leverage his writing. "I began to write articles for some of the seniors' magazines, and they would usually list my company name, phone number, and address with the articles," Robert said. "Also, a couple of magazines did short write-ups on me because my business was so unusual." Both types of articles gave credibility to both Robert and Hawthorne House, he said. He received more inquiries and more jobs from these articles than his display ads ever brought.

Forget what you've heard about the demise of the written word. More than 20,000 magazines are published in the United States alone, and between 800 and 1,000 new ones start each year. Ninety-five percent of them target specialized markets. Millions of Web sites accept articles too. If you or one of your employees can write articles of interest to your target customer, chances are the magazines that target that same audience will consider publishing them. They may even pay you, but at least they should include your name, your company, and how to reach you. Robert determined which publications were most likely to be read by his most probable buyer. Then he studied those publications to find out how his information or articles might fit in. Some publications invite reader participation. Many have new product listings, tips of the month, or industry notes. Often one paragraph elicits greater reader response than a long article.

Business owners who want to write for marketing benefits must keep in mind that the information or articles probably won't be printed if they're nothing more than free ads. The writing that gets published shares new information, tells a dramatic tale, or offers useful tips. Robert wrote about how to trace genealogies, what makes an anecdote interesting, or ten items in your attic that your kids will wonder about after you're gone.

Robert also found ways to expand the benefit he reaped from responses to his articles.

"Every single person who called went on my master mailing list," Robert said. "I mailed regularly to 500 people. If they didn't want their family histories written at the time, they might change their minds later.

Or they might pass on my information to someone they know." After three years in business, Robert added his own newsletter to his marketing writing. He mailed it out three times a year. "It was an excellent, low-cost way to stay in touch with people who had contacted me," Robert said. "One person might not be interested, but might have a sister-in-law who was. I never knew when my newsletter was going to be passed on."

PART 7

THE INTERNET

■ ■ ■

The scientific and military communities started envisioning a network of all the world's computers in the 1950s. But it wasn't until the mid-1990s that the Internet and World Wide Web, which made the Internet user friendly, exploded into widespread commercial use. Many people fooled themselves into believing that the fundamentals of business and economics didn't apply when it came to Internet businesses. Millions of companies with names ending in dot-com rose quickly on hype and disappeared even more quickly when profits failed to materialize.

Even so, e-commerce didn't disappear. Smart businesspeople were creating Internet business models that worked. Of greater significance, traditional businesses began using elements of e-commerce to improve and expand. Today's companies must, at the least, have access to the Internet, e-mail capabilities, and Web sites. Increasingly, they are using this instant, convenient tool to enhance customer service, build communication with employees and suppliers, better reach their target markets, and capture distant markets that wouldn't have been possible even a few years earlier.

If you're starting a business today, you ignore this medium at your peril. Learn to capitalize on its ever-expanding capabilities.

87. BUILD THE BUSINESS FOR THE CUSTOMER

Successful companies respond to customer desires
and needs rather than build what the owner wants.

■ ■ ■

In late 1995, Stanford computer-science Ph.D. candidates Sergey
Brin and Larry Page teamed up to write a paper on a better Internet search
engine. Within months they put their words into action creating BackRub,
a search engine that sought the most relevant Web sites in response to a
search. Competitor search engines relied on the frequency with which
searched words appeared on a Web site. Sergey and Larry thought their
way was better for users. They apparently were right. The search engine,
soon renamed Google, quickly became the most popular in the world,
handling more than 200 million searches each day by 2004. It searched 3
billion Web documents and Usenet messages dating back to 1981. The
brand became synonymous with the industry and computer users trans-
formed Google into a verb meaning to search the Internet for information,
as in, "Google that word."

That original principle—focus on the user and all else will follow—
topped the list of "Ten things Google has found to be true" on the Mountain
View, California, company's Web site. Sergey said that was the most important start-up lesson he and Larry learned in creating Google. "Develop
your product or service with the user in mind," he said. "At Google, we developed the search engine to be fast, comprehensive, relevant, and easy to
use, all things we knew people would appreciate." To provide that result,
the pair maxed out their credit cards to buy a terabyte of data storage while
Google headquarters was still in Larry's college dorm room. As Google's
popularity grew, the company continued to provide what users wanted.
Google staffers working in a collegial atmosphere kept improving the
search engine. To make searches easier, they developed the Google Directory organized by topic, based on Netscape's Open Directory Project. To
satisfy people on the go, Google created Internet search technology for
wireless phones and handheld devices. To accommodate international users, Google introduced versions in ten languages in 2000, adding 78 more

by 2004. To satisfy users who wanted to do a Google search without first going to Google's home page, the firm offered the Google Toolbar. "Our satisfied users and their word-of-mouth endorsements have been our most effective consumer marketing," Sergey said.

The search engine needed more than popularity. It needed to make money. At first Google relied on licensing its technology. But when it decided to sell pay-per-click advertising on its search results pages (Ad-Words) and on other Web sites (AdSense), the company again put the user first, Sergey said. "This lesson was key to our decision to design text-only ads for use on Google. Text ads delivered targeted marketing messages without the distractions of graphical banners or pop-ups. It was the right approach for our users, our advertisers, and, therefore, our business." While competitors tried to require a searcher to use their services, Google continued creating services that attracted users because they were the best, Sergey said. "Users will put up with [forced service use] for a while, but at the first opportunity they'll change."

88. GET A WEB SITE

A Web site can be less expensive and more profitable
than a brick-and-mortar company if you devote the
time and effort to market it correctly.

■ ■ ■

In a way, Ray Allen never stopped his career in advertising that began in New York and Miami. But that was three companies ago. After selling his advertising agency, Ray and his wife Chy moved to Champlain Valley, Vermont, in 1980 to start a tourist attraction, The Vermont Wildflower Farm. That led to a seed and gift catalog company of the same name. They sold the catalog in 1997, but not the rights to sell over the Internet. In 1999, the Internet-based American Meadows, Inc., launched. The catalog later ceased publication.

"Like many small businesses, we created a Web site, but at first it was small. We didn't take orders or even have a shopping cart during the first year," Ray recalled. "Then in early 2000 we created a much larger site to hold all our seed products, information about them, and a full ordering system for credit cards."

When they owned the catalog, they mailed 1.25 million items annually. The major costs were printing and postage. "We spent $12,000 for the Web site in 1999. The beauty of the Web site was that because we didn't have to print and mail the catalog we reduced the price of our products by 50 percent," Ray said. "The Web allowed us to make the product line much bigger. The entire financial dynamic changed. Our Web site was three times the size that our catalog was and had three times the sales at a much lower cost."

Being an old advertising pro, Ray was fascinated by Internet marketing. When his son, Eric, who was American Meadows' Webmaster, touted the importance of signing up with search engines, which was free, Ray couldn't believe it. "I told him that no real advertising is free," Ray said. "But I learned that each search engine had certain rules and if you followed them to the letter, you could get a listing almost always for free. I realized this was something revolutionary. I spent all night submitting to search engines. I spent five months getting a listing on Yahoo!, which our Web development company hadn't been able to do." From those early submissions, American Meadows was listed all over the Internet. Many of those listings remained online for years, although obsolete. The site's Yahoo! listing was also out of date, but after submitting the "change form" 300 times to get the directory to update the listing, Ray gave up.

While Ray didn't have to pay money for these listings, he did pay with his time and advertising expertise. However, as the Internet became increasingly crowded with hundreds of millions of Web sites, Ray, ever the ad guy, started pursuing other ways to drive traffic to AmericanMeadows.com. He discovered paid advertisements through GoTo.com (later renamed Overture) for which he paid only if a potential buyer actually clicked through to his Web site. This form of Internet advertising also allowed him to bid to be listed first when visitors searched on certain words. For example, if he wanted to be the first listing when someone searched on "wildflower seeds" he paid 15 cents or 20 cents for each clickthrough. When the top search engine, Google, introduced the same concept with AdWords, Ray bought key words and got twice the traffic to AmericanMeadows.com than GoTo.com attracted. "I sometimes ran regional campaigns where my AdWords only turned up in, say California, when it was planting season," Ray said. "For those ads my ad usually said 'plant now.' But on regular ads 'free shipping' was a good way to attract visitors."

89. IT'S ONLY A TOOL

Your Web site is not your product. It's one of many tools
for building and running a successful business.

■ ■ ■

Richard Honea worked in just about every job available in the hospitality industry from bellman to manager. As a growing number of corporations and nonprofit groups started contracting out the planning and management of their meetings and conferences, Richard saw a terrific opportunity for an Internet business. That's when the San Diego, California, entrepreneur launched emeetingsource.com. The Web-based service offered to provide meeting planners experienced in handling every detail of setting up meetings, from small board meetings to major conferences anywhere in the world. The company even provided on-site support staff to run the event. "The whole idea [of being Internet-based] was to be available to key accounts at all times," Richard said.

But emeetingsource.com quickly encountered the clash between technology and psychology. While virtually every interaction between company and event planner could be done online, most corporate representatives wanted to talk to a real person. "That's when I realized I shouldn't spend all my time, energy, and money on the Web site," Richard said. "The Internet was only a tool for business, not the business itself."

Many creators of early online businesses invested heavily in technology, online advertising, and other methods to push and pull traffic to their Web sites. Their business models were built around the notion that if their sites attracted enough visitors, profits would follow. Even many venture capital–backed dot-com companies pursued this model into bankruptcy.

"Every company needs a Web site," Richard said. "Just make sure you understand it completely. You must know the lingo. Search engines change weekly to get high rankings. It's a full-time job to stay in the top ten of search results and it's very expensive. Even if your site gets a lot of visitors, a lot of it is junk." In tracking the source of his business, Richard found his Web site provided only about 10 percent of his contracts. "There were so many companies like mine, so much competition," he said.

Richard started treating the Web site as just another element—admittedly an important one—of emeetingsource.com. Instead of spending his entire day driving traffic to the site, he devoted time each day to traditional cold calling. "If prospects wanted to see a brochure, I told them, 'I'll send a brochure but the fastest way to get information about us is to visit the Web site. And if you don't want to talk to me, you can do everything from the Web site.' But most wanted to ask questions, even after visiting the Web site," he said. After Richard adjusted his strategy to a more balanced marketing approach, business grew 50 percent a year.

Richard also discovered that personal contacts with clients, before, during, or after a project, opened the door for more business, something that might not happen from the Web site and e-mail alone. From prospects, he could uncover what bothered them about corporate events and working with event planners. While planning an event, he could solve small problems before they became big ones and even suggest other services that not only increased his profits but also provided a more successful event. After the meeting occurred, Richard could get feedback that could improve the company and ask for referrals from the corporate representative. Many knew others within their company who were responsible for meetings. "Part of our success was from the relationships we had with our clients, and the Web site couldn't build that," Richard said.

90. BUSINESS BASICS STILL APPLY

Many pioneer Internet businesses failed because the owners
thought the basics were different from traditional business.
Successful entrepreneurs know better.

■ ■ ■

Jacques Stambouli came from a family of entrepreneurs on the island nation of Cyprus. His goal in getting his MBA at Harvard College in Boston, Massachusetts, was to learn to be a successful entrepreneur so he would never have to work in the corporate world. For one class, Jacques wrote an analysis of online auctions, best exemplified by individuals on eBay. Jacques's study of online auctions led him to establish ViaTrading.com to buy surplus merchandise and resell it at retail through many different channels.

"The important thing I realized was to remember that a business was a business, whether online or offline. The same balance sheet and the same income statement rules applied," Jacques said. "It was very easy to get tempted by the promise of low overheads that the Internet proposed. A lot of people spend a fortune designing and developing a Web site and then promoting it, rendering any advantage meaningless." He quickly discovered that selling retail online was highly competitive, while selling wholesale online was difficult and cumbersome. The former was easier, but the latter was more profitable. In fact, the secondhand goods market was $100 billion in the United States alone, yet it had less competition. Few wholesalers were providing professional customer service, photographs, and information of the goods for sale, all touches that ViaTrading.com added, along with offline help, if needed.

Jacques stopped selling to individuals and end users and refocused ViaTrading.com resources to the wholesale marketplace. Instead of buying merchandise from brokers and middlemen, he researched how to buy directly from retailers with leftover merchandise to unload, from televisions without the instruction sheet to last season's dresses. That step meant that ViaTrading.com could buy for less. The company started selling only by the carton, pallet, or truckload. It saved money by eliminating the costly processes required to sell to consumers, such as testing each product and repackaging each item.

Many national retail chains had strict guidelines to follow in handling their surplus merchandise, such as removing brand name tags and not advertising the retailer's name when reselling the goods. ViaTrading.com became top-ranked for selling surplus merchandise from its own site as well as through other portals and directories. All of the adjustments were designed to increase efficiency and profitability, exactly as any successful non-Internet business had done for centuries.

"It is important not to get too caught up with your original plan," Jacques said. "The beauty of the Internet is the flexibility it allows. You are not committed to a certain piece of real estate, for example. We rewrote our business plan dozens of times and still it was a work in progress."

91.   PRICING FOR THE INTERNET

Compete on value, not price, when selling Internet services.

■ ■ ■

After more than ten years of management jobs at big corporations, including Honeywell International, Chuck Bankoff decided to start his own Web site design and Internet marketing company, KreativeWebWorks in San Clemente, California, in 1999. He soon discovered that many people shopped for Internet services strictly on price. Having the lowest price was a difficult and dangerous business strategy. Brick-and-mortar firms learned long ago that price shoppers were fickle customers. As soon as a competitor offered something for a penny less, these bargain hunters were gone. However, many new Internet entrepreneurs had to rediscover this basic economic truth. In order to grow KreativeWebWorks into long-term profitability, Chuck speedily realized "All things being equal, the consumer would generally pick the provider with the lowest price. We made sure all things were not equal by offering so much more in terms of superior technology and personal service. We soon found that to maintain the quality product and service we were accustomed to providing we would have to stop competing on price. As it turned out, we discovered that a well-educated consumer will typically opt for value over price."

Chuck devoted a great deal of time and marketing effort to educating potential clients about what value really meant on the Internet. Many of them were setting up Web sites for the first time and had little knowledge about what was available and how to maximize their investment. "Web development was a very mysterious thing to most consumers," he said. Chuck helped potential clients understand the importance of quality on their Web sites by comparisons with familiar items. "You wouldn't show a client a homemade business card printed on flimsy paper. Why would you stake your company's reputation on an amateur Web site?" he asked. Then he helped them understand that effectiveness and return on investment depend on more than attractive graphics and pretty colors. "Having the Cadillac of Web sites was worthless unless your target market could find you."

Once shoppers for Web services looked beyond the price tag, they still had to see value. That's what Chuck stressed on his company's Web site and in marketing presentations. KreativeWebWorks used technical and creative specialists, which gave the Web developer access to exclusive technical and procedural resources not available to "dime-store developers," he explained, adding that KreativeWebWorks' collection of proprietary Web site codes and products "significantly decreased our development time and therefore reduced our development costs." Another way Chuck demonstrated his company's value and expertise was by offering some free products, such as a subscription to *InsideEdge* Webcast series and an e-book, *Amazing Secrets for Profiting from the Internet.*

Although Chuck was competing on value, he carefully managed his own costs so that his prices were in line with the value given. He had strategic alliances with other Web development experts throughout the United States and as far away as Australia, rather than building a large staff whose payroll and benefits would be costly. The alliances also gave him greater flexibility than he could hire in-house to access special skills he could offer clients. "When you're working with designers and programmers in other countries, you have to be careful that their sense of quality and deadlines is like ours," Chuck said. "I always checked references before assigning something to a new person." The relationship benefited the alliance partners as well as giving the client greater value. "As a provider of Internet solutions, we could offer marketing firms, graphic designers, and computer services instant access to the Web industry," he said. "This built their credibility and image and provided them additional income streams while providing us access to their client base."

92. ONLINE CUSTOMER RESEARCH

The Internet provides multiple avenues for
surveying customers and studying competitors.

■ ■ ■

Todd French knew just about everything about stringed musical instruments. Performing since he was five, Todd has been cellist for the

Los Angeles Opera, college recruiter for musical talent, violin restorer, curator of a university's collection of stringed instruments, and head of the fine musical instrument department of international auction house, Butterfield's. When he wanted to start a musical instrument rental service for school children, Todd couldn't find quality instruments at a price that would make the rental business profitable, so he started making the stringed instruments himself in 1995. Although StringWorks in Appleton, Wisconsin, rented some violins, most of the business came from selling the quality instruments. Again, to keep the prices affordable, Todd used direct sales and put StringWorks entirely on the Internet.

StringWorks did more than sell stringed instruments ranging from a $350 violin to a $4,900 cello, it built a community of musicians that trusted the knowledge and helpfulness of StringWorks employees. Todd studied his customers through a discussion board on the StringWorks Web site. "Our customers had a link to their music and instruments that pros didn't," Todd said. "We started a discussion thread, 'Do you name your instrument?' and there were dozens of entries. This was a fantastic way to gain information because people have anonymity on the Web."

Soon, Todd, who was an energetic "multi-preneur," started considering other aspects of the musical instrument market. "One million musical instruments were stolen each year and only 2 percent were recovered," he said. "Those that were found were by chance because there was no identification system in place." So Todd dreamed up, Instrument Security Identification Systems—ISIS for short—to place microchips with unique serial numbers in all types of musical instruments. Music shops would be able to check a national database when someone tried to sell them a musical instrument. The Internet was the perfect place to research what musicians thought of the idea.

"The key was asking the right questions and targeting the right audience," Todd said. He looked for newsgroups, company-sponsored boards, and fan club boards for a wide range of instruments from cellos to trumpets and clarinets. "Once you have found a handful of good message boards or informational Web sites, stick with them and learn about your subject before preparing your survey because many of your questions might be answered already." Todd used five different groups because some sites had wide participation and others virtually none. He asked group members to respond to his survey. "Stay neutral and never require registration, names, e-mail [addresses], or any personal information or you won't get replies,"

Todd advised. He asked 15 questions, but only a few were important to his research. These important questions he placed two-thirds of the way down the list. "Hook people first by making them comfortable, and then they will be more willing to participate and give you the information you really came for." Based on his experience and responses, he rewrote some questions to be more neutral and others to be more specific.

His surveys proved there was a market for ISIS, which Todd launched in 2003, and confirmed what the company should provide. Insurance companies had told Todd that they would like to see a tracking system similar to that used for stolen cars. "But you'd need an electricity source, and no musician would put that on an instrument. It might affect the sound," Todd said. "Sometimes your audience will tell you what you don't need. In one survey, an aspect of the business that I thought was key in success really wasn't. The responses by customers were overwhelming to the negative so I was able to drop it from my business model."

93. THE DILEMMA OF NEW TECHNOLOGY

New technology can differentiate an Internet company
from competitors, but it can also be a stumbling
block in attracting customers.

■ ■ ■

The dream of the paperless office is almost as old as computers. The widespread adoption of the Internet and World Wide Web by businesses seemed perfect to push that dream closer to reality. In fact, iPayables started in Laguna Hills, California, in 1999 as an Internet invoice delivery service with the promise of reducing paper processing costs for large companies. If iPayables could deliver this technology, it would save companies money, reduce mistakes in data entry, eliminate annoyed vendors calling to track their payments, and resolve billing disputes in minutes. Companies should have leaped at the software but they didn't at first, said chief executive Ken Virgin. "The newer the technology, the longer large businesses will wait for a known entity to present it," he said. "Everyone may be excited about new technology, but because it is new and unproven, they want to deal with a company that will be around to clean up the mess if it fails." Even sophisticated financial backers and venture capitalists who claim to want to invest in cutting edge, next-generation technology don't want to get in until the technology is proven, Ken added. "You almost always have to get it off the ground before you can go to venture capitalists."

iPayables customers could direct their suppliers to upload invoices over the Internet. The invoices were electronically matched or routed to the appropriate user for approval. Suppliers could check the status of their invoices 24 hours a day. American Airlines was using another electronic bill-paying system, which didn't work for 17 percent of its invoices. iPayables' system quickly converted those accounts to its Internet solution.

Perhaps because information technology experts launched iPayables, it focused more on superior technology and customer service than on sales and marketing. They worked on training users, implementing the technology, and persuading vendors to adopt the system. That approach helped the company evolve its software and services for greater customer benefit, Ken said. "We obtained some quality early adopters of our technology and we worked hard to make those initiatives an overwhelming success. There may be other methods to capturing a market, but I slept better at night knowing we delivered on what was promised."

These first beta customers were critical to prove iPayables' product, Ken said. But the vast majority of *Fortune* 1,000 companies will always wait for a brand name solution. To accommodate this attitude, iPayables adjusted its business model, moving away from direct sales to customers toward a private-label service solution to develop relationships with established entities to market the technology. In 2003, American Airlines, American Eagle Airlines, and more than 1,500 industry suppliers persuaded the International Air Transport Association to select iPayables technology for its industrywide solution called IATA InvoiceWorks. Other partnerships helped to grow the company and enable it to improve and expand its Internet-based invoicing solutions. "When the time is right and the technology is established, then we will employ our own sales force," Ken said.

94. THE BEST OF TECHNOLOGY AND PEOPLE

Internet profitability requires people with the right combination
of skills and attitude, as well as the right technology.

■ ■ ■

Jason McClain was one of those entrepreneurs whose creative mind works overtime. When he first dipped a toe into the Internet world in the 1990s, he piled e-book sales, e-commerce merchant services, and Web site creation onto his existing graphics and printing company. Soon the Internet possibilities presented greater opportunity for growth, so he sold the graphics and printing side of the business. Jason named his online business PrimeQ Solutions. After the dot-com crash left the image that Internet was synonymous with unprofitability, PrimeQ was a model of the new, New Economy: real profits, no venture capital backing, and flexibility to meet clients' evolving e-commerce needs.

PrimeQ offered a range of performance-based Internet marketing solutions for clients such as mortgage brokers and travel companies. The company created its own technology to generate and track sales leads that had a high close rate because participants signed up to receive the highly targeted information and then verified their interest in a confirmation e-mail. PrimeQ also had an affiliate program that promoted products and brought in leads from more than 10,000 other Web sites. It owned dozens of Web sites that sold information products including college scholarships and estate planning.

The success of these products and services depended on technology, people, and integrity, Jason explained. "First and foremost we took great lengths to make sure that we offered the right technology to ensure accurate reporting, payments, and convenience for our affiliates to work with us. Second, finding the right core group of employees was more precious than gold. I not only looked at experience, skills, and education, but at character and the desire to grow. Third was integrity. I never lied to my staff and always gave the customer what he really wanted." How these three elements work together was illustrated in the way PrimeQ built its vast network of affiliate Web sites that sold products and generated hot leads for which clients were willing to pay. Jason hired a woman who not only had experience building an affiliate network but who had the heart and desire to take the project to the next level. PrimeQ created its own software to track sales by affiliates and aggregate lead generation because affiliates wanted trustworthy data on the amount of activity being performed in order to evaluate the value of PrimeQ's offers. If affiliates didn't receive good commissions, they wouldn't stick around.

"Often affiliates had a narrow focus of our value proposition," Jason said. "Affiliates preferred to be paid a smaller amount on the front end instead of a larger amount on the back end." For example, if an affiliate Web site placed a PrimeQ advertisement for a vacation package, most preferred to be paid $2 for every visitor who requested a sales package than $50 for every visitor who actually bought the vacation package. "In affiliate marketing, it's always the sizzle, not the steak. People buy the sight, smell, sound, and appearance of the offer," he said. "However, if you build your company based on 100 percent sizzle, you might see the dollars begin to roll in initially, but unless the quality is there to back it up, you'll never sustain it."

95. WHAT'S IN A DOMAIN NAME?

Pay attention to details or you could find yourself
unconnected and out of business with no quick recovery.

■ ■ ■

Jeffrey Hunter owned a retail shop in Irvine, California, that sold only neckties. But then he discovered one of the advantages of the Internet: A narrow niche product, like neckties, might not find enough customers in a local community, but it could thrive with the Internet's worldwide reach. Jeffrey first started a Yahoo! store as an adjunct to his brick-and-mortar shop. Within six months, online sales greatly exceeded in-person sales so he closed the shop and became a wholly Internet business. Soon ABC Neckties was selling $10,000 in inventory monthly.

However, Jeffrey got a nasty surprise that nearly ruined his business when he tried to change the domain name service registrar. The Internet Corporation for Assigned Names and Numbers, ICANN for short, accredited more than 100 registrars for domain names ending in .com and .net. They handled tens of millions of transactions daily. Their fees and services varied greatly, and, as e-commerce entrepreneurs like Jeffrey became more familiar with the Internet, they looked for bargains or service packages that better suited their individual needs.

Jeffrey wanted to switch registrar services to get a lower price and better service. When he tried to end his relationship with his old registrar, he was told he had to give 30 days' notice to terminate the service and his annual contract was due to expire in a few days. He objected that he had received no notice about the expiration. The registrar claimed its contact information for him was incorrect. Reluctantly, Jeffrey agreed to renew his registration with the old registrar, and the sales representative gave him a two-week extension to pay the bill. A few days later, Jeffrey, who normally sold hundreds of neckties each week, sold just one tie in two days. The registrar had deactivated http://www.abcneckties.com. Despite numerous frantic phone calls and hours on hold, Jeffrey couldn't get his service reactivated for four days. Then he spent hours relisting with Internet directories and search engines, which were the lifeblood for attracting new customers to his Web site.

This incident wasn't the end of Jeffrey's registrar problems. The next year, he started 70 days in advance to switch registrars. His former registrar sent an e-mail that he didn't have to do anything else. However, at the end of the message was the notification that he did have to reply to the e-mail. It did not provide an activated hyperlink. His new registrar didn't contact him about any problem. Only because of his previous problem did Jeffrey follow up. He had to scramble to make the switch. "I advise people to go in the first place with the company you want to stay with because changing is such a hassle," Jeffrey said.

ICANN tried to end confusion and deceptive practices in the highly competitive registrar arena. For example, domain names used to be resold within five days of an expired registration. Internet pioneers with highly desirable domain names found themselves deleted from the system by questionable tactics. Then ICANN developed a "redemption grace period" of 30 days plus an additional five-day "pending delete" status. These and other experiences like Jeffrey's point out the need for an Internet entrepre-

neur to carefully track registrations and other bureaucracies quickly growing in cyberspace to avoid losing an entire business.

96. EASY AS E-ZINE

An electronic newsletter receives greater, and more positive, feedback from customers than printed versions.

■ ■ ■

Jerry Neitlich understood the importance of staying in touch with
former clients in the commercial real estate industry. A company may use
the services of Jerry's company, In/House Corporate Real Estate in Irvine,
California, once in a decade or more. He wanted to make sure these clients
knew he was still around and still specialized in representing tenants,
rather than landlords. So he decided a newsletter would be one efficient
method of staying in view of these former clients. In 1997, Jerry launched
his monthly newsletter, "Tenant Tactics," printed on heavy, glossy paper
and mailed to clients and colleagues. Soon he moved the publication to
the fax machine, which most business executives owned. Then in 2001,
Jerry moved "Tenant Tactics" online in the form of an e-mailed newsletter, or e-zine.

Not only did the e-zine save money, Jerry could carefully target the
right recipients directly and receive greater notice. "Invariably I got six or
seven calls immediately about issues mentioned in 'Tenant Tactics' or,
best of all, from people I may not have heard from in a while," Jerry said.
"Sometimes I received more than 50 immediate responses ranging from
'Happy Holidays to you too' to 'We need to have lunch and catch up.'
That was definitely better response than mail pieces, faxed forms, or even
the Christmas card that hung at the receptionist's front desk and was for-
gotten."

From the start, Jerry discovered the importance of sending the e-zine
every month so that people anticipated it and recognized the subject line,
which always included the words "Tenant Tactics." Over the years, he
modified and improved both the content and mailing methods for his e-
zine. With the rise of spam and Internet viruses, many people wouldn't

open e-mail attachments, so Jerry pasted his e-zine directly into the body of his e-mails. He discovered that recipients preferred brief e-zines, so he wrote one main story and two short ones on real estate topics of most interest to tenants. "The most important thing was to make the articles relevant. People were always coming up to me at business events to compliment the format and content," Jerry said. "I got a nice compliment from an attorney. A client forwarded him a copy, and he told me, 'You write like you talk, not too technical.' You need positive feedback once in a while."

The most difficult aspect of any electronic mailing program is keeping the address list current. People change e-mail addresses more often than they move offices. Sometimes they notify colleagues and friends of the switch and sometimes they don't. Jerry bought a service to cull his 1,300-name list down to about 750 active e-mail addresses to which "Tenant Tactics" was sent each month. He bought software that placed one recipient's name in the "to" field, much like mail merge software that addressed envelopes to one person. "It was also key that I only sent the e-zine to people I had met. A lot of these types of informational newsletters go out as spam and never get past the delete button." Not only did Jerry hear directly from "Tenant Tactics" recipients, many forwarded an issue to friends. "Many people said, 'I have a friend who is facing this exact issue right now, so I sent him the newsletter. Expect a call from so-and-so.' It was a reliable way to build my business," Jerry said.

97. OPT-IN E-MAIL

Targeted, voluntary e-mail can quickly build your
database of current and potential customers.

■ ■ ■

Christine Kloser had been an entrepreneurial coach, speaker, and writer for nine years when she met four friends for dinner at a Chinese restaurant in April 2000. She knew that women were starting businesses twice as fast as men and yet had different professional and emotional needs. After her Chinese dinner, Christine decided to start Network for

Empowering Women—or NEW Entrepreneurs—in Santa Monica, California, to meet those needs with membership benefits, seminars, a Web site, local chapters, and tele-seminars.

A super networker, Christine initially marketed memberships and seminars through people she met at business or social gatherings. As soon as she set up the Web site, http://www.newentrepreneurs.com, she developed a strategy for getting visitors to agree to receive information about upcoming events and member benefits. The Web site offered a free weekly newsletter to anyone who simply gave a name and e-mail address. Christine promoted this opt-in e-mail database on the Web site, in a business column she wrote for her local newspaper, in online articles, during radio appearances, and networking word of mouth. She even printed the Web site address and information about the free newsletter on the back of her business card.

At first, the Web site didn't make clear the benefits of either subscribing to the newsletter or becoming a paid member of the NEW Entrepreneurs organization. Christine attracted more sign-ups after adding on the Web site that the newsletter had information about free seminars "to help your business grow," savings on business products and services, and helpful articles. If a visitor left the site without signing up for the newsletter, a pop-up box appeared that read: "Wait! Before you leave, take advantage of our FREE "What's NEW" e-zine. Within a year, Christine had 1,500 newsletter subscribers who were also in her electronic database. "Once they were in my database, they usually attended meetings or purchased products, such as seminars and memberships," Christine said. The Web site also pointed out the added value of NEW memberships—value-packed business-building tele-seminars, more than $4,000 in membership benefits, and opportunities for members to promote their businesses. More than 300 women, who were also in the e-mail database, joined NEW during the first year.

While the Internet has become a wonderful source of information and business, entrepreneurs with Web sites and electronic newsletters have to be careful not to be perceived as unwelcome spam. That's why it's so important to get people to sign up for the e-mail voluntarily and to give them opportunities to stop subscribing, usually with a note somewhere in the text of each e-mail or e-zine. People don't linger over long articles on the Internet, so e-zines and e-mails have to have short, yet high-value information. Even announcements stating that you're selling a seminar, book, telephone conference, or membership, must communicate valuable information to retain subscribers.

"I was filling a niche that wasn't served. I helped women entrepreneurs ignite their businesses and fuel their souls," Christine said. "My members were advocates for the organization and newsletter, and they were constantly telling their friends and associates."

98. EBAY BUSINESS

Tens of thousands of people have built full-time
online businesses using eBay auctions.

■ ■ ■

Linda Irish quit working when she had children, but after they started school, the West Covina, California, resident wanted to go back to work. Jobs were scarce in her former career so she started looking around. Her father ran a wholesale business importing statues from the Philippines. Her brother-in-law was a frequent garage sale shopper who turned around and sold many of his purchases on the premier online auction Web site, eBay. Linda decided to blend the two concepts, starting LM Treasures in 2000 to sell some of her father's merchandise on eBay.

The eBay Web site was started in 1995 to provide one place where people worldwide could buy and sell almost anything by means of an auction. Quickly the site grew to tens of millions of registered users with millions of items for sale at any given time. This enormous marketplace proved to be better than any brick-and-mortar shopping mall and better than a stand-alone Web site for many small businesses because it already generated heavy traffic of eager buyers. Also, eBay was simple and inexpensive to use. Within eight years, 150,000 people were making a full-time living from their eBay businesses. LM Treasures was one of them, selling such unusual products as a love seat shaped like a 1959 Cadillac, a ten-foot-long 1957 Chevy wall plaque, and a life-sized plaster cow. "Our store on eBay allowed us to expose our items for a low cost. It was a wonderful marketing tool. We reached customers from all over the world," Linda said.

Start-up was cheap and simple. "I invested in a $300 digital camera and asked my dad if I could take photos of his items and try to sell them on eBay," Linda said. "If an item sold on eBay, I would buy it from him." Though simple, start-up was also a lot of work taking pictures and measuring everything in order to write a compelling description that would lure multiple bidders. In addition, a full-time business needed hundreds of auctions going at once. LM Treasures averaged 300 auctions at one time and sometimes had twice that number. Linda had quite a learning curve as LM Treasures grew little by little. Monitoring that many auctions was time consuming because potential bidders had questions about the merchandise and shipping costs, she said, estimating that she spent more than 40 hours a week on the business. Many of the products were offered strictly for sale, not auction, so potential buyers tried to wheel and deal by e-mail. "There was a lot of correspondence," she said. Shipping was also a learning experience because many of her products were so large. One popular item was a life-sized statue of a chef holding a menu board that restaurateurs bought. "We had to put them on pallets, strap them down, and move them with fork lifts," she said. Monthly sales averaged $15,000 to $20,000. LM Treasures outgrew her garage, so she paid cash for a 2,000-square-foot warehouse. "I was excited as we grew each year," she said.

99. NO BOUNDARIES

Even new online companies can capitalize on the global reach of the Internet to build a vast network of strategic alliances and partners.

■ ■ ■

While earning her law degree, Ana Penn realized the rapidly growing, yet contradictory, worldwide field of laws and regulations governing the Internet and electronic commerce. "Small businesses had to engage in e-commerce, yet they were either unaware of legal and regulatory issues, or they were overwhelmed with conflicting information," Ana said. So she started International Business Law Services (IBLS) in 2000 with offices in Irvine, California, and Brussels, Belgium. The company provided an Internet portal and membership subscription for legal information on e-commerce law worldwide. It also supplied up-to-date e-commerce law instruction. "One crucial aspect to any online business was the need to understand the global audience they were reaching," Ana said. "Along with this reach came the need to understand business strategy from a liability point of view."

Ana needed to develop relationships with experts in many legal specialties and numerous countries in order to satisfy her clients' needs for global information about the Internet and e-commerce law. No one person could know everything. "An e-commerce company may have issues of legal structure, privacy, taxation, intellectual property, cyber-crime. That's five different specialties. Does the company hire five attorneys?" she asked. IBLS's initial thrust was to sign up 70 law firms in 38 countries as charter partners in order to create a database of information about Internet law. This information was sold by subscription to business executives, attorneys, and accountants, and was used in IBLS's online courses in e-commerce law offered through universities' business and law schools. This database enhanced IBLS's image as a source of global Internet law information and training. Its Web site offered articles, such as "Differences in Online Privacy Policies in the United States and European Union." The partner law firms contributed much of the online and subscription material that enhanced the value of IBLS subscriptions.

Companies and their attorneys paid for access to this information in order to deal successfully with increasingly complex interstate and global e-commerce issues. For example, if a Virginia-based Web site sold clothing to a Massachusetts teenager and shipped the products from a Nevada warehouse, which state's laws governed the transaction? Did the retailer owe sales tax? To which state? IBLS's course material explained that Massachusetts had a law to force out-of-state retailers to collect and pay sales tax, but the owner of a small e-commerce site was unlikely to know that. "Because e-commerce often crossed state and national borders, it was generally suggested that the company incorporate on its Web site an explicit clause that the contractual obligations were based on the laws where the company was based," Ana said.

As Internet laws evolved, that kind of information changed, so it was vital for IBLS to rely on its partners. "Credibility is a major issue online," Ana said. "The importance of leveraging relationships with strategically placed companies when starting cannot be overstated."

This strategy paid immediate dividends. In addition to the law firm partners, IBLS started identifying and signing partnership agreements with companies that had synergies with the Internet and e-commerce law content. These agreements enabled IBLS to capitalize on the name recognition of these partners. Furthermore, IBLS subscribers benefited from discounted pricing from these partners available only through IBLS. For example, Bowne Global Solutions, a publicly traded document translation company, became an IBLS partner in order to reach international law firms. As soon as the deal was announced, Bowne's largest competitor contacted IBLS to become a partner as well.

100. BE FLEXIBLE

The Internet has evolved so quickly that online companies must adjust to shifting client needs and demands in order to survive.

■ ■ ■

Custom programming and Internet-based commerce solutions were specialties of Dana Point Communications, Inc., in Dana Point, California. But that wasn't initially the case. Dan and Cindy Busarow started the company in their home in the mid-1990s by offering dial-up Internet connections over local telephone lines. But as technology and client needs changed, so did Dana Point Communications.

The World Wide Web in the late 1990s attracted thousands of new companies with all kinds of products and services. The subsequent dot-com collapse occurred for several reasons, not the least of which was the inability of many firms to make a profit. They either did not listen to customers or could not deliver the products, services, and technologies that these customers demanded. The Busarows made the adjustment. They designed Web sites, but so did thousands of other small firms. Many of those competitors migrated to the Web from graphic design or marketing. They could make Web sites that looked good but many couldn't address the individual needs of their clients. Because the Busarows had both long-time experience with the Internet and expertise in software programming, they were able to deliver when clients wanted customized business-to-business e-commerce solutions.

"The key to success and longevity was using the latest programming technologies," Cindy said. Every Web site client wanted to know, for example, accurate traffic counts, so Dana Point Communications developed a tracking program that was more precise by counting unique visitors rather than page hits. Such customized solutions helped Dana Point Communications differentiate itself from competitors and even form business relationships all over the world. "One of our major clients was in Japan," Cindy said.

One effort to evolve in order to meet customer demand developed into a strategic partnership. Buildingonline.com started as a dial-up customer of Dana Point Communications, Cindy said. Then the Web site firm tapped the Busarows' programming expertise to develop the best search engine for the building industry. "They have become our strategic business partners," she said. "They had a first-rate marketing design team and graphics designer. We did the programming, as well as providing speedy and reliable [Internet] servers." Buildingonline.com delivered more targeted and relevant search results than larger, general-interest search engines because it concentrated on just 200,000 Web sites, updated weekly, that offered products or services for construction, rather than search billions of unrelated sites.

Dana Point Communications also needed to move beyond dial-up Internet access for its ISP clients to high-speed technologies. The partners added other technology services such as local and wide area networks, wireless Internet access, and databases. The Busarows decided that Microsoft Windows solutions weren't as secure and stable as Unix and Linux, so Dana Point Communications concentrated on developing expertise in the latter systems. "They had few system crashes and information loss," Cindy said, "which made happy users who were also satisfied customers." The addition of each specialized service enhanced Dana Point Communications' usefulness to its clients and therefore the company's long-term survivability. "We knew that . . . we couldn't do everything so we keep evolving as business conditions warranted," Cindy said.

101.

REACHING ONLINE DENIZENS

The Internet provides a unique, inexpensive means
of reaching targeted groups of potential customers.

■ ■ ■

Doug Griffith was a Perl programmer, comic book publisher, and a
big fan from day one of Apple computers who realized that Macintosh
owners were a dedicated market for all sorts of products for their desktops
and laptops. Doug and a friend thought one possibility was to create styl-
ish, artistic, even custom panels for Macintosh PowerBooks, iBooks, and
iPods. In 2001, they launched MacSkinz as a part-time, Internet business.
Doug knew standard advertising would not target his most likely customers precisely enough. So he surveyed the Internet for targeted marketing
opportunities. "I checked the logs on my Web site every morning to see
where my visitors were coming from and to determine where people were
talking about us," Doug said. He especially looked for message boards
and user groups where he could hang out and view what special-interest
groups of computer-savvy people were discussing. Message boards or
forums are online gathering places where people with similar interests
share information relevant to a specific topic. Many Web sites include
forums to encourage their visitors to engage in conversation and develop
a sense of community so that they will visit more often. User groups
involve people from all over the world who gather online, in local meetings, or both, to share information and get answers on a common interest.
There were thousands of Apple user groups, for example. While Doug
participated in the Apple message boards and user groups, he didn't limit
his online marketing to this segment.

"I frequented every message board I could find related to our product
and mentioned new designs and sometimes offered a 20 percent discount
to the message board members," Doug said. "I was on a Ferrari message
board, and people were wishing for a red computer to match their cars. I
did a mock-up of a MacSkinz that looked like a red Ferrari and uploaded
it to that message board with the note, 'We can do this for you.' It was a
huge hit." At any given time, Doug dealt with 20 different message boards

that he checked daily. "Sometimes I had to defend myself. Sometimes I gave instructions. I always signed my messages with my [Web site address] so they could contact me," he explained.

These message boards and user groups were highly sensitive to self-promotion and free advertising. Doug found hundreds of relevant user groups, but when he tried to post information and the 20 percent discount offer for MacSkinz, participants told him to quit spamming. "Especially the head of the group didn't want such posts. But some of them said if I went through them, they would confirm my information, filter it, and send my verified message to the whole group," he said. One group that sent out the message had 500,000 members.

Any Internet marketer must be keenly aware of anti-spamming and anti-commercialism attitudes of people online. Doug's use of his Web site address in his signature and an illustration in response to posters' requests tended to be acceptable. But it's wise to be a silent observer on message boards and online user groups for a while to determine their tolerance for messages about products or services.

PART 8

START-UP GUIDE

■ ■ ■

While the real experiences of real business owners in the previous sections are insightful guides, they may not explain all the details you need to consider when you start your own business. This section contains some nuts and bolts to move you through the process more quickly, point out tasks you might not think of, and encourage you to start efficiently, yet correctly.

ARE YOU CUT OUT TO BE AN ENTREPRENEUR?

Many people think about starting a business for many different reasons: anger at a boss, layoff from a job, desire for more control over life. While such motives often provide the impetus to start a business, they aren't enough to sustain a business or create a successful business owner. Most small-business owners start out with skill in the technical side of their venture. However, technical skill is just the beginning.

Consider how you like to work and the types of work you enjoy. A business owner must be a multitasker: He must make the product, create marketing materials, send out invoices and follow up when customers don't pay, strategize for future growth, and find the best financing deals. None of this is rocket science. But it's not easy either.

Successful entrepreneurs are thick skinned, independent, and able to forego instant gratification. They focus on how to achieve something, not on the obstacles in the way.

Here are some questions to ask yourself about your abilities and motives for seeking business ownership. Be honest. No one has to see your answers but you. However, you have to live with the consequences if your dishonesty or wishful thinking persuades you to start a business you hate or are unprepared to run.

- Are you prepared to lose your savings?
- Do you know what your strengths and weaknesses are?
- Do you have the drive, persistence, and ambition to achieve and grow?
- Are you completely committed and determined to attain your goals?
- Do you strive for excellence?
- Do you have a high level of self-confidence?
- Are you a hard worker?
- Do you have a tolerance for ambiguity, stress, and uncertainty?
- Do you have a low need for status and power?
- Do you get along well with others?
- Are you good at communicating?
- Are you trustworthy and reliable?
- Are you patient?
- Are you well organized?

- Do you carefully read and understand important documents before signing them?
- Do you understand basic math and know how to read financial statements?
- Are you creative and innovative?
- Can you live within a budget?
- Do you have good health and a high energy?
- Are you willing to accept complete responsibility for yourself and your business?

If most of your answers are yes, you're ready emotionally to start your business. But don't count yourself out if you have some no or maybe answers. You may be able to overcome those areas with experience, formal study, or help from people with strengths in your weak spots.

Other considerations arise if you plan on running your business from home, as more than half the start-ups do. Answer these questions about yourself:

- Are you a self-starter?
- Can you stick to business if you're working at home, avoiding chatty neighbors, and dealing with unruly kids?
- Do you have the necessary self-discipline to maintain schedules?
- Can you deal with the isolation of working from home?

WHAT BUSINESS SHOULD I START?

Some people know what business they will start before considering their own ability to start or run it; others just know they're burning to be an entrepreneur and must find the right venture. But even if you think you know what business to start, you should hone the idea into a profitable niche. The classic rule is to find a need and fill it. That's easier said than done.

If you have no idea what type of business you want to operate or even what industry is appealing, your search will begin with a few questions.

- What do you do well enough that people will pay for?
- What do you like to do well enough that you'll happily do it ten hours a day, five or six days a week for years on end?
- What new technology or service is just starting to take off?

- What hobbies or interests do you have that are marketable?
- What product or service does your community lack and why?
- Of what have you recently said, "I sure wish I could get a good _____ (fill in the blank)."?
- Where do you want to live? (If you want to live in Florida, you'll have to abandon that dream to run a snowplow rental shop.)
- Can you deliver a better service or one of higher quality than others are providing?

Think about potential businesses that match your answers. Ask your family and friends to brainstorm with you. At first, don't allow any negative reactions, such as "that won't work." You want as many ideas as possible before you narrow your choices.

If you already have a potential business in mind or come up with some likely candidates through brainstorming, ask a few questions about that business.

- How much competition will there be in your chosen location?
- Can you bring special skills or proprietary information to that business to give it a competitive advantage?
- How can you add value to a basic idea to make it even better?
- What are the major expenses and what are your resources?
- What are the primary risks in that type of business and how can you minimize them?
- Would such a business satisfy your goals and values?
- Would you be proud to tell your mom that you own such a business?
- Will your local government allow such a business in your chosen location and if not, where could you operate such a business?
- Can you create a demand for the business you have in mind?
- Are there potential detrimental environmental effects in the business?
- Is there something about this business that hinders effective marketing?
- Can you make a living in such a business?

Your final decision will be to choose the business that you are able and willing to do, that fills an unmet need in the marketplace, that can make sufficient profits for your needs, and that you have the time and capital to start.

MONEY SOURCES

One of the most common questions asked of the U.S. Small Business Administration's toll-free Answer Desk (1-800-UASK-SBA) is "Where can I get a grant to start my business?" An SBA spokesman replies, "If such grants existed, I wouldn't be here, I'd be out starting my own business." Yet lack of capital is one of the major reasons entrepreneurs give for not starting the business of their dreams, and undercapitalization is one of the major causes of business failure. So where else can you get the money you need to start your business?

Yourself

The source of start-up capital for more than eight out of ten enterprises is personal funds. That can mean savings, credit cards, home-equity loan, loan against a life insurance policy, or 401(k) retirement account. Many fledgling business owners sell off something of value, such as a coin collection, an antique car, rental property, or the family's sterling silver.

Relatives and Friends

The second most common sources of start-up financing are the people who know you best and trust you most. If you can't persuade your parents or best friends to invest in your venture, how will you persuade strangers?

Suppliers

Usually, suppliers of raw materials to new companies want cash up front. However, some suppliers will extend you credit so you can pay for supplies out of the sales of your first products. Perhaps they know and trust you, based on previous business relationships. You may need a good business plan to convince them of your firm's viability, and they may want a long-term, exclusive contract for "investing" in your start-up.

Customers

If you have customers before you start business, they may be willing pay in advance so you have some money to get started. Many start-ups even have their former employer as their first customer. If they won't pay 100 percent in advance, they might be willing to pay half in advance and the rest on delivery instead of in 30 days to help your cash flow in the beginning.

Asset-Based Loans and Factoring

Once you have accounts receivable (customers who owe you money), you can either borrow against the amount owed or sell the accounts. The former is called asset-based lending and the latter is called factoring. The arrangement is based on the creditworthiness of your customers, not you, so even new companies can use this source of working capital.

Factoring is expensive. First, the factor will charge 4 percent to 6 percent on a 30-day invoice. Second, it will only pay you a portion, typically 50 percent to 90 percent, of the face value of your receivables up front on the possibility that the bill might never be paid.

A factor may use aggressive collection tactics with your customers that might hurt your relationship with them. An asset-based lender won't do that, because collections from customers and payments to the lender are your responsibility.

Line of Credit

If you have a good credit history or equity in your home, some lenders will set up a personal line of credit from which you can borrow to pay initial bills. It is unlikely that a fledgling business will get a line of credit without the owner's personal guarantee. The business itself may not qualify for a line of credit for two to three years.

Commercial Loan

Banks and other commercial lenders are unenthusiastic participants in the business start-up game. Unless you're applying for a home-equity loan—which really equals personal funds (note that it's listed in the first category in this chapter)—lenders usually want to see two to three years of profitable experience of a business before they part with any of their depositors' cash. This is true even of loans guaranteed by the U.S. Small Business Administration. The lender wants to see collateral, an ability to repay the loan, and the owner's experience in the industry. However, some new ventures do obtain bank loans. They have a well thought out, written business plan that spells out how the loan will be repaid. The owners have experience in the industry, excellent personal credit histories, and collateral.

Small Business Innovation Research (SBIR) Grants

Okay, so there are *some* grants for start-ups. In the SBIR program, government agencies that have research and development budgets—such as the Department of Defense—award some money to entrepreneurs to try to prove the viability of new technology for specific needs of the government. Check with the SBA, which oversees the program.

Venture Capital

Venture capital comes from limited partnership pools managed by experienced investment managers. These funds are looking for investments that are likely to return at least 40 percent on investment annually or higher and go public or sell to a larger company within five to seven years. Only a few thousand companies get venture capital each year. The most important factor venture capitalists look at is a strong management team. A good business plan is also essential.

Private Investors or Angels

Private investors usually get into a company at an earlier stage with smaller investments than venture capitalists, but angels are also looking for high-growth companies. They have industries in which they are most comfortable investing. Many want to take out their investments within five to seven years. Some are willing to sit on the sidelines and let the management team run the company, but others want to take an active role in management.

Strategic Partners

You might find another company willing to enter into a joint venture or strategic partnership with you or license your product or technology. Partnering works best when each participant has something the other lacks. You might have technology that would take others years to perfect. They might have established markets, distribution channels, management expertise, or money.

WHEN BORROWING IS YOUR CHOICE

If borrowing is a viable and desirable financing approach for your small business, a few steps will make the process go more smoothly and take less time. Not all lenders are the same. Shop around and have the self-confidence to realize that you can be a good customer for some institution. The lender should be a good partner for you too. Ask these questions:

- What is the total cost of the loan (including interest rate, terms, fees, points, and prepayment penalty)? A low introductory rate could hide the true cost of the loan over time if you don't read carefully.
- Does the length of the loan match the purpose for the money? You don't want to be paying off a loan long after the equipment you bought with the money has worn out.
- What qualifications does the lender require of you?
- How long will this lender's application process take?
- Is the lender knowledgeable about and comfortable with your industry and the type of loan your business needs?
- Does this lender have the ability to make the kind of loan or lease you need?
- Are you comfortable with this lender? Do you trust him or her?

What does a lender want from you? A lender will be looking for equity, collateral, your experience in the business or industry into which you are venturing, good credit, and ability to repay the loan. A typical loan application will require certain business documents.

- History of the business and purpose of loan
- Financial statements (three years for an existing business). If this is a new business, you will have to provide past personal income

tax returns. Realistic, pro forma financial statements for the new business will be helpful to show how the bank will be repaid.

- Schedule of term debts for an existing business or for you personally if this is a new business
- Aging of accounts receivable and payable for an existing business
- Projected opening day balance sheet for new business
- Copy of lease
- Amount owner(s) have invested in the firm and personal financial statements for each
- Résumés for all owners and officers. Bankers like to know with whom they're doing business.

FORMS OF BUSINESS OWNERSHIP

When organizing a new business, you need to choose the ownership structure. The basic choices of business ownership are sole proprietorship, partnership, and corporation. Each form of ownership has advantages and disadvantages. Your choice usually will depend in part on the number of owners of the business. You can't, for example, choose sole proprietorship when you have six owners.

You're not stuck with a chosen form of ownership forever. As your business matures, the initial choice of a business structure, no matter how well it performed in the start-up phase, may require adjustment or alteration. However, it can be time consuming to the change ownership structure, so give careful thought to your start-up choice.

Sole Proprietorship

This is the easiest and least costly way of starting a business. You can form a sole proprietorship by finding a location and opening the doors for business. You will have few expenses other than business name registration, a fictitious name certificate, and other necessary licenses. You may not need an attorney, and you, as the sole owner, have absolute authority over all business decisions.

The downside is that the owner has unlimited liability for all business debts, which may exceed total investment in the business. If the owner becomes ill, is disabled, or dies, the business ends.

Partnership

If a business has more than one owner, the most common choice of ownership traditionally has been a partnership. (This has changed somewhat with some of the modified corporations now allowed by law for small businesses.) The two most common types of partnerships are general and limited. A general partnership can be formed simply by an oral agreement between two or more persons, but a legal partnership agreement drawn up by an attorney is recommended. Legal fees for drawing up a partnership agreement may be lower than incorporating.

Corporation

A business may incorporate without an attorney, but legal advice is recommended. The corporate structure is usually the most complex and usually costs more to organize than the other two business forms. Control depends on stock ownership. The holders of the largest stock ownership, not the total number of shareholders, control the corporation. With control of stock shares or 51 percent of stock, a person or group is able to make policy decisions. Control is exercised through regular board of directors meetings and annual stockholders meetings. You must keep minutes to document board decisions. Small, closely held corporations can operate more informally, but record keeping cannot be eliminated entirely. Officers of a corporation can be liable to stockholders for improper actions. Liability is generally limited to stock ownership, except where fraud is involved. You may want to incorporate as a C or S corporation.

An S corporation provides the liability protection of stockholders, but does not pay taxes like a C corporation. Instead, taxable income, losses, deductions, and credits are passed through to the corporation's stockholders. The individual may pay a lower tax rate than the corporation would. (Ask your tax advisor for the current federal and state tax rates.)

Limited Liability Company

In addition to the three major forms of business structures, most states allow limited liability companies (LLC). An LLC is similar to and taxed as a partnership, and it offers the benefit of limited liability for individual owners like corporations and S corporations. This limited liability protects you from legal and financial liability if the business fails or loses a lawsuit. Unlike S corporations, LLCs don't have some of the limits on the number and status of ownership.

WHERE TO LOCATE YOUR BUSINESS

The wrong location can kill a fledgling business faster than almost any other decision. But the right location is more than its geography. Fledgling business owners have so many options: Home or high-rise, suburbs or downtown, shopping center or mixed-use area, and now, the Internet.

The factors that are critical to your location choice vary with the type of business. For a manufacturer, cost of land, availability of labor, and proximity to freeways or railroads may be important. For retailers, visibility and large population base may be key factors. For services, population plus image may be crucial. Here are some potential questions to consider.

- Whom are your potential customers and where do they live or work?
- Where do your employees live?
- If you're looking at a specific site, does the surrounding community need your product or service? Does the site have enough foot and vehicle traffic to help your business? Restaurants and retailers need more traffic than manufacturers.
- Is the area growing or declining? What is the future?
- How accessible is the potential location?
- If you make deliveries or have sales representatives, how convenient is freeway access?
- Are surrounding businesses compatible with your company but not direct competitors?
- Does the location meet current needs with flexibility for future growth?
- How well are similar businesses nearby doing?
- Do city zoning and other ordinances allow your type of business in the chosen location? What about sign laws for that location?
- What kinds of amenities does the site have, such as affordable restaurants for employees or hotels for out-of-town clients?
- Does parking and security meet the needs of your customers and employees?

- Do the site and the city project the image you want for your business?
- Can you pay the rent and still make a profit?

WRITE YOUR BUSINESS PLAN

A written business plan will be the most important work you do in preparing to open a new business. It will direct your start-up and growth, help you obtain loans or investors, focus the direction of your company, and guide basic decisions about running your business. Your business will never be too large, old, or successful to benefit from a written plan. While books, software, and consultants are helpful, write the plan yourself so that you will be intimately familiar with the details of running your business. This personal involvement will be especially important if you must make presentations to lenders, investors, strategic partners, or customers.

Keep the plan on your computer so it can be changed easily as circumstances evolve. Keep a printed copy in a loose-leaf notebook so pages can be replaced. Above all, use the plan. Too many entrepreneurs write a business plan when they start and never look at it again.

Format for Your Business Plan

If the business plan is just for you, it won't matter what it looks like. But lenders and investors will expect your plan to follow a format that contains these general headings:

- Title Page
- Executive Summary
- Table of Contents
- The Business
- Marketing
- Financial Analysis
- Operations
- Supporting Documents

The title page, or cover sheet, should contain the name of company, its street address, telephone number, and Web site address; the names, titles, and contact information for all owners and officers; the date the plan was prepared; and the name of the person who prepared it.

The executive summary, although placed in the beginning of the plan, is written last and pulls everything together. It summarizes what the business does, where it's heading, how it will get there, and why it will succeed.

The table of contents makes it easier to find information within the document.

The business section describes the enterprise and its goals. It states the legal structure, responsibilities of key executives, competitive advantages, protections in place for intellectual property, location, methods of distribution, and hours of operation.

The marketing section describes your products or services, identifies the customer demand, details the size and location of your target market, and explains how you will attract and increase market share. This section also briefly describes your pricing strategy and methods for advertising.

In the financial analysis, you describe the sources and amount of your initial capital. In this section you should project your monthly operating budget (income and expenses) for the first year; identify your break-even point, expected return on investment, and monthly cash flow for the first year; include a projected balance sheet of assets and liabilities; and address contingency plans if unexpected problems develop. Many experienced entrepreneurs include three versions of the budget: optimistic, expected, and worst-case scenario.

The operations section explains how the business will be managed day to day. Discuss hiring and personnel procedures. List the insurance, lease, or rental agreements, but put copies of the actual documents in the next section. List the equipment necessary to produce your products or services. Describe production and delivery of products and services.

The supporting documents section should contain details of the previous sections, such as partnership agreement or articles of incorporation; pro forma profit and loss statements; copies of leases for your building, office space, retail shop, equipment, etc.; and copies of your business license and other legal documents.

Marketing Plan

In addition to the general marketing section of your business plan, you want to have a detailed marketing plan for each product or service. You will also create a separate plan for each marketing campaign. If you're not marketing, your business won't succeed. Also, the better you plan, the more effective your marketing will be. You will save time and money. Without a plan, the tendency is to try a little networking over here, and then run an ad there without knowing whether it will sell anything. A basic marketing plan includes sections regarding:

- *Executive summary.* As in the business plan, this summary outlines the marketing you will do and why.
- *Your company.* Define your pricing strategy (i.e., low-price leader). Describe your position in the market (i.e., best value, highest service). Detail how you will distribute your product or service.
- *Product or service.* Define what you're selling, your market research, and your competitive advantage. Being as good as competitors won't work. Describe the benefits to the customers. Answer their question: What's in it for me?
- *Customer.* Describe the market niche or segment you are targeting and the people most likely to buy from you.
- *Competition.* Identify who else is after the same consumer dollar. It might be direct competitors (you sell soda and so do they) or indirect ones (they sell water, beer, iced tea). Candidly explain why customers buy from them. Detail or estimate their sales and market share.
- *Other obstacles.* Describe other hurdles that prevent customers from buying from you, such as the fact that you can't get your product into stores or it lacks name recognition.
- *Opportunities.* Explain how you'll overcome obstacles. "I don't have enough money, but I do have strong relationships with *XYZ* buyers and a dedicated and tireless sales force."
- *Goal.* What do you want to achieve, especially over the next three to five years. Be specific.
- *Strategy.* Detail the plan of action or system for achieving your long-range objectives. If the goal is to increase profits, the strategy might be to attract more high-wealth clients.
- *Tactics or tools.* Identify the specific means to achieve your strategy and goals. If you want to attract more high-wealth clients you might offer top quality, extra service, and home delivery.
- *People.* Assign specific people to be responsible for each action. These people can be independent contractors as well as employees.

- *Calendar.* Set dates to accomplish each event or activity. Be specific. Review this calendar at least monthly to evaluate if you are on track or if a scheduled activity needs to be modified.
- *Budget.* Set aside the specific amount of money, time, staffing, etc., you will devote to each marketing activity.
- *Supporting documents.* These should include market research reports, customer surveys, competitor evaluation sheets, and market trends.

PRICING A PRODUCT OR SERVICE

While pricing is part of marketing, it's worthy of being in a separate section because it's difficult for most newcomers to determine. The price of your product or service must be between two points: what the customer is willing to pay, and your breakeven point (the point at which you start losing money). Setting price is part art and part science, and there are several factors that go into the development of an optimum price.

Here are the steps to follow to ensure your price is right.

1. Develop a pricing strategy.
2. Develop a goal for your pricing strategy.
3. Learn what your competitors and colleagues charge.
4. Calculate your costs and determine how much you need to make.
5. Identify your added value.

Pricing strategy determines your position in the range between the customer's price ceiling and your profit floor. Do you choose a higher price and possibly sell fewer products or do you chose a lower price and aim for higher volume? Remember, it's difficult to raise prices later because you've already told customers what the product is worth. If you offer the same exact product under the same conditions to different customers at different prices, you could run afoul of the law. But you can offer different prices for different conditions, such as mail order versus store purchases. You also can package products and/or services, which could help move slow-selling items or sell more of these items than you would separately. Also decide if you want to give volume discounts. If you're selling a service, you must decide whether to charge by the hour or the project. Some clients have a preference. You should have sound reasoning for your pricing strategy.

What's your goal? Remember that pricing is a strategic tool, so it should be in tune with your marketing strategy and the way you are positioning your products. If you are aiming to be the Rolls Royce of your industry, you will make your products out of the finest materials, pay meticulous attention to every detail, establish 24-hour customer service, and offer a no-questions-asked return policy. If you're positioning the same product for struggling newlyweds, you'll use good but not perfect materials, assure that the product won't fall apart but perhaps not endure to the end of the millennium, provide assistance from 10 AM to 4 PM Monday through Friday, and accept returns with a receipt.

Learning what competitors charge is easier than it used to be, if you're willing to do some online research. Many small-business owners are happy to post their typical fees or share information with colleagues who don't serve the same geographic markets. Also, some industry publications publish membership surveys that include this information. You can even get competitive information by interviewing some target customers. You might tell them you are developing your business and ask them what they would expect to pay, or typically do pay, for the types of products and services you'll be offering.

Of course, you'll calculate your costs. Charging less than your costs is a quick road to bankruptcy. Don't overlook indirect costs, such as utilities, marketing, and taxes.

Identify your added value. You might be able to increase your prices if you add value for customers. What are they willing to pay more to obtain: Free delivery? Higher quality? Immediate access?

FIND HELP TO MAKE A GOOD BUSINESS BETTER

Assistance comes in many forms. You may need employees immediately, although the majority of start-ups don't. The United States has three times more enterprises without employees than with employees. But even a new business owner with no employees needs outside assistance including:

- *Attorney.* New business owners need someone to give them legal advice, read over contracts, and evaluate a partnership agreement or articles of incorporation.
- *Accountant.* Also helpful is someone to review your financial records and prepare the company's quarterly taxes.

- *Contractors.* If you plan to make and sell products or food items, you will need the help of a contract manufacturer.
- *Services.* You may need assistance making brochures, designing a logo, servicing your computers, or printing your marketing materials.
- *Independent contractors.* If you need help with a specific project, an independent contractor can provide expertise that you may not possess. When the project is done, you are not obligated to continue the relationship.

If you use independent contractors be careful not to treat them like employees. Here are some of the Internal Revenue Service guidelines.

- Avoid telling them how to do the work, where to work, and what hours to work.
- Give them broad guidelines and state your desired outcome, but don't instruct them how to do the work, which helpers to use, what equipment to use, or what sequence to follow.
- Do not train them to do the required work.
- Hire for a specific project or period of time, not indefinitely.
- Pay by the project, not the hour. Ask them to include businesses expenses in the bid. Don't pay for them specifically and separately.
- Assure that they have other clients.
- Prepare a written contract.

None of these issues is a concern if the contractor's business is incorporated, because legally, you're hiring an entity not a person.

Some businesses may need to hire employees from the start. You also will need an IRS tax identification number and possibly a separate state employer identification number. Be aware of all the costs of an employee, which can add 25 percent to 50 percent to base pay. Law requires some of these expenses, such as worker's compensation insurance, Social Security, Medicare, and federal and state unemployment taxes. Other costs may be necessary to be competitive in the job market, such as paid vacations, paid holidays, bonuses, uniforms, supplies, and health insurance.

Before you hire, write a job description so you know what you're looking for. Establish performance measures so employees know what is expected of them, what they can do to help the company, and how they can advance their careers.

While interviewing job candidates, focus on the applicant's skills, experiences, and education. If you look at the applicant's appearance and behavior, make sure you are seeking clues to traits that are desirable for the job rather than unrelated issues, such as age or race, which could make you vulnerable to a charge of illegal discrimination. Don't do all the talking. The more an applicant talks, the more he or she reveals.

Document everything about an employee and his performance from the time of application forward. A written record of both good and bad occurrences will help you improve the employee's performance and give you grounds to fire him, if necessary.

Develop written policies and an employee handbook. These policies will establish how work gets done in your business, convey the philosophy that drives your business, and emphasize the importance of the employee to achieving success. The handbook should answer questions employees frequently ask. Avoid words like *must* that will limit your discretion in disciplining and firing employees. If you include lists, such as causes for firing, make it clear that these are examples and not all-inclusive lists. Whatever rules you set in the handbook must be followed to avoid employment lawsuits later.

One good source of help that many new business owners fail to employ is a banking relationship. You may be tempted to save a few dollars in bank fees by using your personal bank account for business dealings. Don't. The business should have its own account: to verify spending that is tax-deductible if done for business purposes, but not deductible if done for personal use (this is important if the IRS audits your returns); to satisfy some creditors and suppliers who want to see a business name on checks; and to prevent comingling of business and personal spending. In addition, a business bank account helps you psychologically view your company as a real business and yourself as a real business owner.

Most banks will require certain information before opening a business account, including:

- Proof of the business's legal status, such as a fictitious name statement or articles of incorporation
- Two pieces of identification, including one that bears your photo, such as a driver's license or state-issued ID card
- IRS tax identification number (sole proprietors can use their Social Security number)
- Minimum initial deposit, usually $500 to $1,000

RECORD KEEPING

You must keep accurate financial records for your new business to succeed. However, many fledgling entrepreneurs just open their doors without setting up a system to track finances. They determine the business financial health by the amount of cash in the bank. But well-kept financial records are essential when it's time to file your income tax returns. Also, the government may audit certain types of businesses, such as retailers to verify the accuracy of sales, and use tax returns or determine if tax is due if a return has not been filed. These records also are helpful when you apply for business credit from a supplier or a loan from a bank. More important, these financial records show you at a glance how your business is doing.

Small business owners must keep a variety of records, some for legal or tax purposes, some to assist them in managing their business. Records you should keep include:

- *Business checkbook.* Your company should have a bank account separate from your personal one.
- *Budget.* This should outline in detail your anticipated spending and income.
- *General journal of transactions.* This should list all debits and credits by date.
- *General ledger.* This should track your company's income, spending, assets, and liabilities, generated from the general journal entries.
- *Petty cash record.* This should be a record of all business-related expenses paid in cash. If you buy lightbulbs for your home-based business while at the grocery store, write it down and keep the receipt.
- *Accounts receivable* (what customers owe you)
- *Accounts payable* (your company's bills)
- *Inventory.* Keep separate inventories of finished goods, materials, and supplies.
- *Payroll records* (if you have employees)
- *Mileage log/travel and entertainment record.* Record the date, location, and business reason for each expense.
- *Customer records.* These should include the customer's name, address, and phone number; the type of service provided or product bought; any guarantees given; and the terms of agreement.

These records help you keep your balance sheet and income statement.

To create a balance sheet, list all assets—cash, equipment, inventory—on one side of the paper, and all liabilities—original investment, leases, debts, expenses, taxes—and owners equity on the other side. The totals of each side should be equal.

An income statement lists all revenues, cost of goods sold, and other costs and expenses. You hope that after all the costs are deducted from revenues, you'll have some profit left over.

Set up your system to track all sources of money, property, and other income and separate business and nonbusiness income. Track which sources of income are taxable and nontaxable. Also track all business expenses that are tax deductible, such as some equipment purchases and business travel. Record the details of each asset, such as the purchase date and what percentage of its use is for business. Such information is needed to calculate gain or loss if you sell an asset or it is destroyed. Keep records of depreciable assets. If you sell an asset or make capital improvements to one, only a permanent record shows how much of its cost you have recovered.

These documents can help you analyze your business. For example, look at cash on hand at the beginning of the month and at the end. If the latter number is higher, you're on the right track. Calculate the gross profit margin for each product or service (subtract the cost of materials from net sales). You'll spot unprofitable items quickly. Your quick ratio will show if you have liquidity or cash-flow problems. Calculate it by adding all your cash, short-term investments, and current receivables and divide by all your current liabilities.

Legally, you must keep sales and use tax records for four years unless the overseeing government agency gives written authorization for earlier destruction. This rule applies to all records that pertain to transactions involving sales or use tax liability.

In addition, if your company is audited, you should keep all records until the audit is completed (or all appeals are final). Retailers should also keep certificates from buyers to document claimed nontaxable sales. If you can't prove that you sold to someone with a valid resale permit, you may have to pay tax, interest, and penalty charges.

START-UP CHECKLIST

Thousands of tasks arise as you plan and launch your new business. This checklist outlines the basics.

- Understand the responsibilities/benefits of business ownership.
- Evaluate your strengths, list your weaknesses, and set goals.
- Choose the business you want to start.
- Obtain any training, education, licensing, or accreditation you need.
- Apply for needed trademarks, patents, and copyrights.
- Decide which form of ownership your business will have.
- Write a budget and decide how much money you will need for the first year.
- Write a business plan.
- Research your market.
- Define your niche.
- Identify your most likely customer.
- Determine how to handle distribution.
- Develop a marketing plan.
- Choose your location and sign a lease, if necessary.
- Apply for a fictitious business name.
- Retailers obtain a resale license.
- Obtain a tax identification number from the Internal Revenue Service.
- Apply for a city business license or home occupation permit, if needed.
- Reserve a Web site domain name.
- Set up financial records.
- Establish an ongoing relationship with an accountant.
- Open a business bank account.
- Obtain a merchant account for accepting credit card payments.
- Buy necessary business insurance.
- Order business cards and stationery.

In addition, your business may require various documents, licenses, or other items, depending on what kind of business you start, where it's located, and how it operates. Some common documents include:

- Fictitious name statement (often called a DBA for "doing business as") usually issued by the county government
- Work certificate or a vocational license from the state
- Tax identification number from Internal Revenue Service if your business will have employees. (You are responsible for withholding income and Social Security taxes, and being in compliance with minimum wage, employee health, and safety laws.) Some states require a separate state tax identification number.
- Domain name for Web site address
- Resale permit from the state (so you don't have to pay sales tax on products you buy to resell to customers)
- Merchant account and machinery to accept payment by credit card from a bank, often sold through brokers and agents
- City business license. This may be required by the city in which the business is located *and* by cities in which certain businesses do work, such as the work remodelers, landscapers, and seminar providers do in cities other than the one in which they are established.
- Home occupation permit for home-based business. Some cities issue this permit instead of or in addition to the business license.
- Zoning: confirm that your city or county government allows your proposed business at your chosen location
- Certificate of occupancy from the local government for a commercial location
- Fire department safety inspection by city or local fire jurisdiction
- Police permit through the local police agency (for some businesses, like gun sales)
- Sign permit from city or county
- Incorporation, limited liability company, or partnership or limited partnership from the state, usually the Secretary of State Corporate Filing Department
- Trademark from U.S. Patent and Trademark Office. You can also register your company name with the state government, especially if you do no interstate work.
- Patent or copyright from the U.S. Patent and Trademark Office
- Business bank account from a commercial bank
- Workers' compensation insurance through a private insurance carrier

- Health permit to make and sell food, usually regulated by the state, but oversight may be delegated to county health departments
- General contractor's license for builders through the state licensing board
- Alcohol seller's license through the state alcohol control board
- Federal Occupational Safety and Health Administration safety permits that apply to your business or location

INTERNET RESOURCE GUIDE

Government

- *Census Bureau* (http://www.census.gov). Provides plenty of economic and demographic reports. Click on news and then census briefs to reach full reports for your area.
- *Federal government* (http://www.business.gov). Includes information in one place for all federal sites helpful to businesses.
- *National Technology Transfer Center* (http://www.nttc.edu). Includes information about the center, which provides technical assistance and grant opportunities; information about assistance from the Department of Defense, NASA, and small-business development centers; inventors' resources; and technical briefs.
- *Service Corps of Retired Executive*s (http://www.score.org). Includes useful information from SCORE's volunteer counselors plus success stories.
- *U.S. Patent and Trademark Office* (http://www.uspto.gov). Provides a wealth of information about how to search for existing patents and apply for new patents, as well as filing fees.
- *U.S. Small Business Administration* (http://www.sba.gov). Includes information on starting, financing, and running a small business; many programs for small businesses; links to other useful government sites.

Associations

- *National Association for the Self-Employed* (http://www.nase.org). Provides legislative updates, articles from *Self-Employed America* magazine, and a reference section.

- *National Federation of Independent Business* (http://www.nfibon line.com). Reports on legislative action on bills that affect small businesses and other news from this Washington D.C.–based lobbying group.
- *Center for Women's Business Research* (http://www.nfwbo.org). Provides data on women business owners and studies of women entrepreneurs' work habits, based on research done by the foundation for the National Association of Women Business Owners.
- *American Association of Franchisees & Dealers* (http://www.aafd. org). Provides tips, programs, and publications for franchisees.
- *International Franchise Association* (http://www.franchise.org). Includes resources, government issues, and other information for franchisers, franchisees, and people considering either role.

Publications

- *Dearborn Trade Publishing* (www.dearborn.com). Publishes small-business, entrepreneurial, and real estate books.
- Entrepreneur *magazine* (http://www.entrepreneur.com). Publishes thousands of useful articles about starting and running a business.
- Inc. *magazine* (http://www.inc.com).Web site archives past articles from *Inc.,* and provides bulletin boards, interactive worksheets, and help in creating a Web site for your business.
- *Nolo Press* (www.nolo.com). Publishes do-it-yourself legal books; Web site provides hundreds of tips and articles for small-business owners.

WEB SITES OF THE BUSINESSES PROFILED IN THIS BOOK

(The number indicates the chapter in which each company is mentioned.)

1. Wendy's International (http://www.wendys.com)
2. Sarris Candies (http://www.sarriscandies.com)
3. Kinkos (http://www.kinkos.com)
4. Creedon Controls (http://www.creedoncontrols.com)
9. Janie Williams & Associates (http://www.jwandassociates.com)
10. Carolina PetSpace (http://www.petspace.citysearch.com)
12. EagleRider Motorcycle Rental (http://www.eaglerider.com)
13. Laurey's Catering (http://www.laureysyum.com)
15. People Dynamics (http://www.thedynamicsgroup.com)
16. Pampered Chef (http://www.pamperedchef.com)
18. 1-888-Inn-Seek (http://www.innseekers.com)
19. NoUVIR Research (http://www.nouvir.com)
20. Blackburn Manufacturing (http://www.blackburnflag.com)
21. Martin Integrated (http://www.martinintegrated.com)
22. ECI (http://www.e-c-i.com)
23. Home Teams (http://www.hometeamsla.com)
25. Omni Tech (http://www.otcwi.com)
26. Mills/James Productions (http://www.millsjames.com)
28. Kott Koatings (http://www.kottkoatings.com)
29. Ohm Corporation (http://www.ohmcorp.com)
30. Lillian Vernon (http://www.lillianvernon.com)
31. Diversified Investigations LLC (http://www.diinv.com)

34. Direct Effectz (http://www.directeffectz.com)

35. Hsu's Gensing Enterprises (http://www.hsuginseng.com)

37. Coffee Beanery (franchising company) (http://www.coffee beanery.com)

40. Fitness International (http://www.fitnessinternational.com)

41. Southwest Financial Services, Inc. (http://www.sffinancial group.com)

42. Royce Technologies (http://www.royceinst.com)

44. Rainbow Station (http://www.rainbowstation.org)

45. Nikken (http://www.nikken.com)

46. Training Dynamics (http://www.consultapc.org/sherkow.htm)

47. Cross Timbers Innovations (http://www.roadstervalet.com)

48. Power-Fill (http://www.power-fill.com)

49. Carl's Jr. (http://www.carlsjr.com)

50. JMG Security Systems (http://www.jmgsecurity.com)

52. Employers of America (http://www.employerhelp.org)

53. Rowena's, Inc. (http://www.rowenas.com)

54. Zet-Tek (http://www.zet-tek.com)

55. GenCorp Consulting (http://www.gencorpconsulting.com)

57. Haas Outdoors, Inc. (http://www.mossyoak.com)

58. Wright-K Technology (http://www.wright-k.com)

59. Outback Steakhouse (http://www.outback.com)

60. Sisters & Brothers, Inc. (http://www.freshdressings.com)

61. Painten Place (http://www.paintenplace.net)

62. Harvest Time Foods (http://www.annesdumplings.com)

63. Sorensen Moving & Storage (http://www.sorensen-allied.com)

64. Telephone Doctor (http://www.teldoc.com)

65. Lontos Sales & Motivation (http://www.prpr.net)

66. Rudy Salem Staffing Services (http://www.rudysalem.com)

68. Badmoon Books (http://www.badmoonbooks.com)

71. Diana's Cookies (http://www.californiacookies.com)

72. Site-b Company (http://www.squirrelmixer.com)

74. Optiva Corp. (http://www.optiva.com)

76. PDQ Personnel Services (http://www.pdqcareers.com)

77. Information Management Resources, Inc. (http://www.imri.com)

78. Global Strategies (http://www.globalstrategies.net)

79. Roberts Management Solutions LLC (http://www.robertsmgmt .com)

80. Venture Outdoors (http://www.venout.com)

81. InterScience, Inc. (http://www.intersci.com)

83. Rich Mar Shirts & Signs (http://www.richmarsigns.com)

85. Yarn & Company Financial (http://www.sdeanyarn.com)

87. Google (http://www.google.com)

88. American Meadows (http://www.americanmeadows.com)

89. emeetingsource.com (http://www.emeetingsource.com)

90. ViaTrading.com (http://www.viatrading.com)

91. KreativeWebWorks (http://www.kreativewebworks.com)

92. StringWorks (http://www.stringworks.com)

93. iPayables (http://www.ipayables.com)

94. PrimeQ Solutions (http://www.primeq.com)

95. ABC Neckties (http://www.abcneckties.com)

96. In/House Corporate Real Estate (http://www.inhousecorp.com)

97. Network for Empowering Women (NEW Entrepreneurs) (http://www.newentrepreneurs.com)

98. LM Treasures (http://stores.ebay.com/lmtreasures)

99. International Business Law Services (http://www.ibls.com)

100. Dana Point Communications (http://www.beach.net)

101. MacSkinz (http://www.macskinz.com)

INDEX

A

ABC Neckties, 171–72
Accountants, 111, 199
Accounts payable, 202
Accounts receivable, 189, 202
Accreditation, 144
AdSense, 160
Adventure travel, 145–46
Advertising
    direct mail, 150–51
    web sites, 160–62
Advisors, board of, 131–32
AdWords, 160, 161
Alcohol seller's license, 206
Allen, Chy, 160
Allen, Eric, 161
Allen, Ray, 160–62
Alliances, 85–86
Allied Van Lines, 115–16
Alternative Board, The (TAB), 111
Amazing Secrets for Profiting from the Internet, 166
American Airlines, 169
American Meadows Inc., 160–62
American Society for Quality, 143
Americans with Disabilities Act, 120
Anderson, Nancy, 46
Anderson, Terry, 45–47
Angels, 190
Another Alternative, 136–38
Antonia Korby Design, Inc., 126–27
Apple Computers, 127
As-if principle, 83
Asset-based loans, 189
Associated Enterprises, Ltd., 61
Association of Professional Consultants, 87
Attorneys, 111, 193, 199
Audits, 202, 203
Auto Valet, The, 88

B

BackRub, 159
Badmoon Books, 123–24
Bailey, Carl, 62–63
Balance sheets, 57–58, 203
Bank accounts, 205
Bankers, cultivating relationships with, 11, 61, 111, 201
Bankoff, Chuck, 165–66
Bankruptcy, 24–25
Barney, Sue, 145–46
Barrow, Michael, 124–25
Basham, Bob, 109–10
BBL (Beyond Bottom Line) Forums, 111
Berkshire Hathaway, 32
Better mousetrap myth, 135–36
Blackburn, Bud, 37
Blackburn, Jim, 37–38
Blackburn Manufacturing, 37–38
Board of advisors, 131–32
Bonefish Grills, 110
Bowne Global Solutions, 179
Brin, Sergey, 159–60
Brong, Gerald, 24–26
Brown, Jeffery, 21–23
Budgets, 76, 202
Buildingonline.com, 180
Busarow, Cindy, 179–80
Busarow, Dan, 179–80
Bush, Barbara, 58

deductions, 201, 203
income tax returns, 202
tax identification number, 200, 201, 204, 205
TEC, 111
Technology
Internet and, 168–71
investment in, 47–49
Telephone directories, 149
Telephone Doctor, 116–17
"Tenant Tactics," 173–74
Texas Instruments, 10
Theft, 92
Thomas, Dave, 3–4
Thompson, Larry, 68–69
Todaro, Diana, 127–29
Tracy, Brian, 95
Trademark, 205
Training Dynamics, 86–88
Transactions, journal of, 202
Travel and entertainment record, 202
Trust, 124–25

U

Unemployment taxes, 200
Uniform Franchise Offering Circular, 51
Unix, 180
U.S. Department of Commerce, 52
U.S. Patent and Trademark Office, 205
U.S. Small Business Administration, 8, 188, 190
User groups, 181–82

V

Value, 165–66
Venture capital, 78–79, 190
Venture Outdoors, 145–46
Vermont Wildflower Farm, 160
Vernon, Lillian, 57–58
ViaTrading.com, 164

Virgin, Ken, 168
Visibility
public speaking/seminars, 153–54
signage, 151–52
Vision, 9
Vocational license, 205

W

Waters, Meg, 121–22
Waters and Faubel, 121–22
Weatherline, Inc., 116
Web sites, 160–63
see also Internet
domain name, 205
Wendy's International, 3–4
West Coast Asset Management Inc., 7
White, Pearl, 148–49
Williams, Janie, 16–18
Woo, James, 146–48
Work certificate, 205
Workers' compensation insurance, 200, 205
World Wide Web. *See* Internet
Wozniak, Stephen, 126–27
Wright, Dale, 105–6
Wright-K Technology, 106–7

Y

Yarn, Karen, 154
Yarn, Steve, 153–54
Yarn & Company Financial, 153–54
Yobs, Richard, 112–13

Z

Zakaryan, Jeff, 141–43
ZelnickMedia, 58
Zet-Tek, 99–100
Zettler, Dan, 99–100
Ziglar, Zig, 95
Zoning, 17, 194, 205

Share the message!

Bulk discounts
Discounts start at only 10 copies. Save up to 55% off retail price.

Custom publishing
Private label a cover with your organization's name and logo. Or, tailor information to your needs with a custom pamphlet that highlights specific chapters.

Ancillaries
Workshop outlines, videos, and other products are available on select titles.

Dynamic speakers
Engaging authors are available to share their expertise and insight at your event.

Call Dearborn Trade Special Sales at 1-800-245-BOOK (2665) or e-mail trade@dearborn.com

Dearborn™
Trade Publishing
A **Kaplan Professional** Company